The House
Kathleen Lightfoot

smith|doorstop

Published 2014 by
smith|doorstop Books
The Poetry Business
Bank Street Arts
32-40 Bank Street
Sheffield S1 2DS
www.poetrybusiness.co.uk

ISBN 978-1-910367-10-0

Typeset by Utter
Printed by printondemand.com
Author photo: Bob Lightfoot

smith|doorstop Books is a member of Inpress,
www.inpressbooks.co.uk. Distributed by Central Books Ltd.,
99 Wallis Road, London E9 5LN.

Supported by
**ARTS COUNCIL
ENGLAND**

The Poetry Business is an Arts Council National Portfolio
Organisation

Contents

New Worlds

The Delivery

To My dear Margaret
with love and best
wishes for the future
Kathleen Ajot
22-7-2014.

For my family, with love

House

The Quiet House

There had been four children, three boys and one girl, who had lived with their parents in that small stooped house. The house seemed an intruder, alien, the only one to be seen on that flat, unending land. Sliced by dykes and drains, the earth was parched in summer, its soil turned to a dust that eddied at the least whisper of a breeze, up into that huge sky. In autumn the rains brought a thick, claggy, soil, too heavy for a man to walk on or to plough. The biting wind of winter carried ice on its tail, that laid an opaque cataract on the still water in dyke and drain. It turned the land into a hard linoleum, crackling and splintering with every footstep. And over it all, in every season, that high, soaring, enveloping sky.

School was unknown to the children. Every hand no matter how small was needed to coax a living out of the soil. It was more important to walk a straight furrow behind the plough than the five straight miles to school. They knew each other well, each other's thoughts and foibles, without realising it. They were the quiet children of quiet parents. This was not to say that they were uneducated or knew nothing. Bible stories were their fairy tales, hymns their nursery rhymes and a straight non-conformist path was their way to salvation.

Their toys were provided by nature. Animals roughly whittled out of small pieces of wood. A doll, in reality more an impression of a doll, gouged out of a palm-sized piece of wood, was the girl's constant companion. All were shared and treasured by the children. As they grew older the fields and hedgerows were still their playground. Small round pebbles levered out of the fields and thrown into a circle scraped out of the soil provided long hours of entertainment. From a young age the boys became adept at using a catapult, and that brought many a rook or pigeon to add to their meagre food.

They could read the sky, the clouds, the differing winds. They knew every bird by its local name, its plumage, its eggs, its voice. They observed every flower, where it grew and what insects plundered its nectar. The life, mating, birth and death of the beasts the family possessed were hardly remarked on. It was part of the yearly cycle that was their life, they knew no different. Christmas was a name to them and a half remembered carol from their mother's childhood. Their festivals were the quarter days when their father travelled to the small market town to pay the rent and sell at the market. They would hear him in the dark, loading the ancient shallow boat: first the pitifully few eggs in a nest of grass and leaves placed in the centre, then surrounded by whatever food the family could find from the land. Snared rabbits, earth-tasting fish from the dykes, both kept fresh with dock leaves, a couple of cabbages, a dozen apples, blackberries, wild garlic, or mushrooms all picked by the children. Any produce that could be sold, that would pay the rent and buy the basic flour, salt and oatmeal that they needed to live. If there was a penny or two left over, their father took pleasure in carrying back a handful of toffee for the children and a twist of thick blue paper with a spoonful or two of tea nestling in it for his wife.

It was a hard life for both man and beast, but a hard and lonely life for the women in the family. In 1912 both mother and daughter took ill. When they could no longer care for each other, the men shouldered the task. Unseen by anyone apart from their family they wasted. The old plough horse made two long slow journeys to the churchyard in the distant village. What noise, chatter and laughter there had been in the family was buried with the women.

In 1914 the news of the outbreak of war took some weeks to drift along the tracts and dykes to the house. They knew that as agricultural workers they would never be called upon to serve in the ranks. The eldest boy, peasant to the core, knew that the tenancy of the land would be his one day, and stayed with his hand on the plough guarding his inheritance. The younger boys, knowing they would always be menial labourers here, couldn't kick the soil from their boots quickly enough and enlisted.

The cultivated land shrank as the ageing man and his son attempted the Herculean task of trying to do the work of four men. Apart from glancing at the sky and deciding on that day's weather they spoke little. The dykes and ditches became ever more choked as the years passed. The neglected fields slowly crept over track and path, merging one with another until they became a wilderness, inhabited by rabbits and their predators.

The day came when they saw movement in the far distance, on the horizon. They stood together, silent, watching the black dot moving, sometimes having to back track along unfamiliar paths. At last they could recognise the postman's small pony and trap. They walked to meet him, They handed back the buff coloured envelope and asked him to read it to them.

A son and brother had died, drowned, unnoticed, in the thick mud of another flat field, under another huge sky, in another country.

The father took the paper into his stained hands and inclined his head in thanks. They both turned and started the long walk back. Each was locked into his own thoughts and neither a word was uttered nor tear was shed.

The old man lived long enough to see his youngest son return from the war. The eldest son felt an overwhelming sense of relief that his brother had returned. This soon faded when he realised that his brother's mind and emotions had been shredded in the war machine.

There was an unchanging stillness to their days, broken only by the soft, slow movement of harness, the plaintive cry of birds and the screams of war that rolled perpetually in a tormented head. The elder brother would glance up from his task and see the old horse, head bent, standing quietly before the machinery and his brother absent. At first he would search for his brother, inevitably finding him cowering in a dyke with his head pressed into the bank, and sobs racking his skeletal body. In time he stopped searching for him until the evening light started to fade.

If their days were silent often their nights were rent with cries and sobs as a war was relived. He would hold his brother's hand and sit, listening to experiences he could never comprehend.

For many weeks the dark gunmetal sky had rained incessantly. It had flattened the furrows, it turned the earth into a thick, sinking glue that sucked and brought both man and horse to a standstill.

Each day his brother pulled more and more into himself. Unwashed, silent, head bowed, not moving, his eyes gazing blankly into another world. It was as if he had wrapped himself tighter and tighter in the darkness of the sky and rain. Then the morning came when he had become increasingly agitated, walking, touching, his movements repetitive, compulsive. His voice muttering and whispering to himself, his ears closed to every other sound. The evening came and he had gone.

With a sack flung over his head and shoulders, a storm lantern in one hand and a stout stick in the other, the elder brother had begun to search. Within seconds the mud was locked on to his feet, his legs sank into the quagmire. The rain soaked his skin and his clothes clung sodden and heavy against his body. He battled to his brother's nearest sanctuary, and found it empty. He peered through the curtain of rain and could see nothing. The sky was dead. No stars, no light to help his search. He cursed his brother, then cursed the war that had left his brother still trapped in it. The stick sank deep as he leaned on it trying to wrench his feet out of the mud and start his search again. He stumbled on, cold, shivering and hunched against the rain. The flickering flame of the lantern seemed to create more shadows on the ground than it dispelled. Yet he knew that he couldn't give up, that he couldn't abandon his brother.

Then he saw something, or did he? Was it a deeper shadow thrown by the lantern, or an irregularity in that mud? Every fibre of his body ached, every part of his body and soul prayed that it was his brother and that his search was over. He lurched forward and sank to his knees. He touched the shadow and knew that it was his brother and that his brother was dead. But so much of his body was not visible. His face was lost, sunk deep in the thick sticky mud. His hands and arms were reduced to a dim outline in the brown ooze. His brother's body was slowly sinking, He frantically scooped and pushed into the mud searching for the familiar face until at last his fingers could locate the nose, mouth and the chin. The mud resisted his hands, it moved and sucked as he probed deeper into it. At last he felt hardness and was able to slip his hands around his brother's head and he struggled to lift it clear. With his thumbs he gently eased the mud from the closed eyelids. With the cuff of his sleeve he carefully wiped the mouth. The dim glimmer of light from the lantern showed him the streaks of wet earth remaining on the face and the dark soft mud in the nostril. He stroked his fingers lightly down them and mud slid slowly out and on to his fingers. The rain washed over the dead face, it streamed off the sack covered head and shoulders of the remaining brother and pooled where he knelt. His brother was dead. There was nothing more he could do for him. Gently, almost reverently, he laid his brother's head in the mud and watched as it gradually disappeared. He rose, turned and slowly made his way home to the silent, empty house.

The Empty House

I t was the big open sky that appealed to me, that and the fact that when they released me after eighteen months in the sanatorium, I was advised to live somewhere dry with clean air. We couldn't afford Switzerland so my doctor father said go east. I was thrilled as visions of Egypt and Palestine swam before my eyes. I was quickly brought down to earth as he laughingly said, East Anglia, dear girl, East Anglia.

I had been cosseted for too long. My mother continuously hovered over me, eat this, time for a rest, wrap up warm. After all it was 1938, I was thirty years of age and it was more than time I stood on my own two feet and besides I felt ready for an adventure. My father and I studied the maps and decided on a small town that I could use as a centre in my search for a cottage. He gave me a wink and declared that he would dream up a crisis to prevent mother from coming with me, otherwise I would never find anywhere suitable in her eyes. Father and I had conspired on many occasions.

I was waved off at the railway station like royalty. After changing trains twice during the journey, each change bringing a slower, stop-at-every-halt train, I arrived at the small market town. It was delightful, totally different to the large industrial town I had left seven hours before. The sun glinted on small flint houses, blanket stitches of red bricks highlighting their windows and doors. A squat towered church guarded the crossroads and as I started to walk towards it, I could see a market cross and the public house that kept it company. A sprinkling of shops and family businesses, locked and silent, waited in the quiet street for morning. Their names were strange to me. Tricklebank and Threadgold, like names from a fairytale. And P. Orviss esq. Land Agent.

Then thankfully I saw a bed and breakfast sign in the front window of a cottage.

I was the first caller at the land agent's office the next morning. Agriculture was in the doldrums and there was a surfeit of farms and cottages on long or short leases and, more importantly, they were cheap. Over the following week I travelled by bus and train all over the area. Tiny hamlets, solitary decrepit houses, cottages with their thatch alive with mice. But there was no cottage that spoke to me, none that said 'I'm waiting just for you'. Yet I knew that I wanted to make my home here, I wanted to live under that magnificent changing sky. I was dejected and decided that my only option was to get the map out again.

A courtesy visit to thank Mr Orviss proved to be my salvation. There was one cottage, empty for nearly a decade, isolated, not suitable for a lady, especially a single one. Perhaps he should have mentioned it before, but had doubts that he should mention it now.

I laughed, I'm a believer in fate, and asked for the keys and directions. He was uneasy and it was obvious he regretted telling me. He turned his ruler over and over as he stared into space.

Suddenly he looked at me, thumped shut a gigantic ledger, locked the door of the key cabinet and said I'll take you.

I stumbled out, Oh I couldn't, too much trouble, thank you, and all the usual words we don't mean. I had a feeling, call it a premonition, that my search was ending.

He pinned a card on the door: Back later.

I smiled, no mention of how much later. In the yard he manoeuvred a pony between the shafts of a neat trap, helped me into it and we were off.

The roads and lanes were narrow and I held my breath when we occasionally passed another vehicle, but before long we turned onto the paths and tracks that edged the fields and dykes. The further we travelled the less habitation we saw and the more uncultivated and neglected the land. We crissed and crossed dykes and paths, raggedy and overgrown. I had seen nothing like it, I was captivated. The air was dry, the sky stretched to eternity and birds soared, calling to the clouds. Then, what had been a hiccup in the horizon started to take substance and as we trundled nearer it grew into a cottage that hugged the earth. The sky was like a blanket enfolding it, tucking itself around the corners, between the chimney pots, around the thatch and the rickety lean-to sprouting from the end wall. It was like a baby, minute, lost in its swaddling blanket.

The pony clip-clopped into the yard and we both sat, staring at the neglected cottage and land. I must admit, although I had been warned, the reality took my breath away. My throat suddenly went dry, tightening, as if I were choking. Tears gathered, my spirits dropped. I struggled to drag a deep breath into my lungs and told myself not to be a defeatist and what had I said about fate. A few seconds later I was standing in front of the wooden door. He slipped the iron key into the lock and after some scraping and a great deal of leverage it reluctantly turned. The door did not swing open to welcome us, instead it stayed tightly shut. A kick from his heavy boot soon solved that problem!

A stale, shut up, dusty, mouse smell leaked out and I stepped straight into the room. I peered, trying to see through the still brown gloom. Cobwebbed windows were framed by perished curtains, hanging like strands of stained bandages. The walls were discoloured and stained, the plaster crazed and loose in patches. There was some furniture, comfortless, plain, home made. Wooden straight backed chairs, a small settle, a scrub top table and a shelf. A carpet of undisturbed dust muffled my footsteps on the stone slab floor. A small cast iron range, dull and blotched with rust was set into a wall. The oven door opened easily despite the crust of corrosion on its hinges. My eyes were held, that's odd, the kettle was on the grate with a small heap of grey ash beneath it. It's as if someone had been making a cup of tea and had popped out for milk. I glanced at the agent, his eyes slid past me. On the mantle shelf were two odd candlesticks, the candles yellow with age, the drips spilling down on to the shelf and half eaten by mice. The same fate had been dealt to a box of matches, their faded heads were spread like polka dots along the shelf. I inspected the scullery: a single-paned window, a plank door complete with two coats hanging from two nails, and a brown slop stone without a tap. Before I could speak, Mr Orviss said

Spring and rain water. The pump's out the back.

I asked to see upstairs and thought I was dreaming or had been transported into another country. There was no staircase. There was however a ladder which disappeared through the ceiling. I stared in disbelief. Why would someone dismantle the staircase, I asked? They haven't, was the reply. The house was as it had been built over a hundred years ago. Farm cottages had always been built this way around here. The man of the house would pull the ladder up on going to bed and let it down, anchoring it on its hooks, in the morning. Oh how little I knew. Gingerly, clutching the stiles with tight hooked fingers, I took a deep breath and started. One foot, two feet, together, rest. Like a child I edged up the ladder until my head was level with the opening, one more rung and I could see along the dusty floorboards of the bedroom. I could make out a bed with frayed rope lashed from side to side and a thin mattress sagging through it. A rough wooden stool stood at the side. A small plank door was ajar in the far wall, the gloom so deep it was impossible to pierce it. I crept down the ladder and looked around the room. I was convinced that I could be happy here even if it did resemble a landlocked Marie Celeste.

I'll take it.

Mr Orviss was aghast.

Did I know about earth privies? No, but no doubt I could learn.

Did I know how to light or cook on a wood burning fire, could I even cook?

I thought of home and Mary the cook, Ethel the maid. I had never cooked, washed a dish or a dress and had never been awake when a fire was lit. I was ready to learn, but from whom, I didn't know. Was there anyone here willing to live in such isolation, never mind willing to teach me such diverse skills? For the first time I felt doubt, I questioned my capabilities. My eyes strayed past the dust and grime and followed the shaft of sunlight, out through the open door, along the packed earth path as it stretched towards the horizon. It was at that moment that I knew that this is where I wanted to be.

It's strange the furniture being left, I mused.

The land agent didn't reply, he seemed preoccupied.

I will rent it on a long term lease and the furniture included if possible.

He nodded, glanced at me, cleared his throat, and slid his finger around his shirt collar.

There is someone. Young but very sensible, very capable. I think she may be willing to come and live here.

I was stunned, I hadn't thought of losing my independence before I had even gained it.

She's my eldest daughter, fifteen years old and can run any household.

Why not, I thought.

If you would care to call into the office at one o'clock tomorrow, the lease will be ready for signing and my daughter will be there too.

I was ready to start a new chapter in my life. Little did I realise the challenges, adventures and friendships I would encounter along the way.

The Contented House

I made two momentous decisions that day in 1938. The first was to take the tenancy of a cottage and land that had been abandoned ten years before. The second was to employ Phyllis and it would have a major impact on my life. Years later I still find it difficult to describe her job. Housekeeper, handywoman, dairymaid, smallholder, teacher, companion, friend. All of these and more besides.

I had no intention of employing anyone when I viewed the cottage with the land agent. With a few probing questions he had quickly highlighted my many inadequacies. I could understand his reservations. I knew nothing about living in the country, had been in hospital for eighteen months, and although there was an intriguing hint of mystery about the cottage, it was dark, dirty and decrepit. He tentatively suggested help from his eldest child Phyllis. 'Rising fifteen and very good in the house' is how he described her. 'She'll work hard for her keep and a few coppers a week'. She's nothing but a child I thought. I was soon to realise that this child had a woman's head on her shoulders, and there were times when I wondered if she had ever been a child.

She sat quietly on that first day as her Pa went through his list. Workmen were already checking the thatch, the chimney and the well. They would make sure the earth privy was sound, whatever that meant. The overgrown grasses and bushes near the house would be hacked back. The rest was up to me.

It wasn't long before Phyllis's questions revealed that my observational skills were nil. I shrank into my collar as I admitted that I had not noticed brushes, buckets nor firewood in the cottage. When I remarked that I loved watching the sky and didn't want curtains at the windows, the glance she gave her Pa clearly asked, is this woman mad?

It was arranged that I would open an account with the only hardware shop in the town. We were ushered in, escorted to seats and offered tea. New account customers were rare. Most of their trade was in pennyworths of nails or new brush heads. It was obvious that they intended keeping our business. I still can't believe the pleasure we got from buying cleaning equipment. All to be delivered by half past eight the following morning at Phyllis' insistence.

The dawn sky was a pale, pearly blue when the trap drew up and I was slotted between baskets, boxes, Phyllis and her Pa. I could hear movement from two of the wooden boxes.

It's only the cat and dog I've borrowed. They'll shift the vermin was her reply to the question I hadn't asked.

Within minutes of arriving at the cottage every window and door was open. The damp, half eaten mattresses had been pushed through the upstairs window and piled high ready to be burnt. It wasn't long before curtains and coats were added and it still wasn't delivery time. Phyllis had brought rough sacking aprons and calico caps for us both and we needed them. In a moment she was covered in grey dust as she tried to clear the heap of ash from the fireplace. She was determined to get a fire lit for hot water and then the hard work could start, she maintained. I quaked in my shoes.

It was soon obvious that I had no idea how to do or organise housework. It was months before I realised the difficult situation I had put this girl in. She rose to the occasion. I was courteously dispatched to see if there was firewood or logs in the barn. My screams brought her running. There were rats running in all directions. A few seconds later a dog and cat were deposited in there, the doors shut and there they stayed all day. Soon a fire was lit, every battered pan we could find was filled and found a place on that fire. A huge black, sooty, kettle that I couldn't lift was filled and sat on the hob, slowly warming. We were ready for the tools to arrive.

There was no time to rest or admire them. It had been explained to me in detail how to clean a room and upstairs was my starting ground. At mid-day we rested in the sun and feasted on bread, cheese and a bottle of cold tea.

Every morning we arrived, every evening before we left, the cat and dog were locked into the house. At last the day came when every floor, every stick of furniture, every door, everything, had been scrubbed more than once, the old walls had been given four coats of whitewash and we were delighted and proud of ourselves.

For the hundredth time, I wondered at the hidden history of the cottage. But this time I actually voiced it. Phyllis's head shot up, her startled eyes stared into mine. I knew then that she could unlock some if not all of the mystery. I also knew that she didn't want to and I would need some mighty powers of persuasion to prise the story out of her. There was plenty of time.

Oh, how busy living in the country turned out to be. Phyllis was always devising plans to feed us, save us money, earn us money, see us through the winter. Then she would have a word with her Pa when he called. I suppose it was part of his work to know the happening on the farms that he was agent for and what surpluses they had. Before long we were the owners of chickens, hens, an elderly milk cow, half a dozen ducks, a pig and three big wooden beehives complete with bees which terrified me. Each day was full and we lived by nature's clock. We rose with the dawn and went to bed with the night.

It was while we were having a bedtime cup of cocoa after a tiring but satisfying day that the mystery started to be unravelled. I had just turned the wireless off and we were idly chatting about Herr Hitler and all the talk of war. I remarked that I was against any war and thought that the senseless slaughter in the last one would stop it being repeated. Phyllis took a sip from her cup and said:

One of the brothers who lived here was killed in the Great War.

I looked up, Who told you that?

Pa, and he said another one came back with his brain addled.

How many brothers were there?

Three I think.

Any sisters?

Don't know.

Where are they all now, what happened to them?

I don't know much about them. Halkon was their name and I only know that because it's on the war memorial. It's the only family name on it that I don't know. Nobody seems to know them, apart from Pa, and the seed merchant and the grocer, not that they bought much from him. Everybody had forgotten about them until you came.

Ma told me that they didn't come to pay their rent one quarter day, but they weren't the only ones, a lot of tenants hadn't. It had been a wet summer, the harvest ruined, then a wet autumn, followed by an even wetter winter. Miles of fields were under water and you couldn't get around the land without a boat, so it was weeks before Pa got out to the farm. He told Ma that he knew something was wrong when he turned off the track. There was no smoke from the chimney and he started to see dead chickens in the flood water. The door to the cottage was unlocked. There were two plates of food on the table, all dried up and covered in mould. He reckoned cabbage and mash. Ma always thought it strange that Pa noticed this, because he can never tell you what he's eaten.

I smiled encouragingly, willing her to go on. I wanted to know everything and quickly before she regretted starting the tale.

Pa told her that everywhere was damp, there was water beaded on the walls and the floor was shiny with moisture. He said his heart was in his mouth and he was shaking with fear when he climbed the ladder.

Our eyes turned towards it. We climbed the ladder with our eyes, we felt his apprehension. I held my breath. I didn't know the outcome. Phyllis did. My eyes swivelled back to her.

He clambered into the bedroom. Nothing, it was empty. He dreaded opening the other bedroom door. It was empty, but the beds had blankets on them, the pillows had head hollows in them. That left just the barn and the land. Pa said he wished he'd never come when he slithered through the mud to the barn. He didn't want to go in, he peered through a crack in the door trying to see anything that would stop him having to open the door, but the gloom was too deep. He told Ma that all he wanted to do was turn around and run home. What he did do, was push the door open and walk in.

He found him inside, hanging from a beam where he'd been for weeks. Pa said he had fight to stop himself from being sick. He looked for the other brother in the barn, around the house, in the near fields and dykes, nothing. Pa couldn't get home quick enough. He told the police, they spent days searching the land for the brother, looking for any clues as to where he was. Again nothing. He was never seen again.

If you ask me, there was murder done here.

I was shocked and speechless. All my romantic ideas had been demolished.

For days it was constantly in my mind. I hesitated before going into the barn, putting myself in Pa's shoes and trying to imagine what he'd seen that day. But life goes on.

We were so busy with the livestock and the extra land. It was at odd times I would think of them. Did they keep fowl and plant potatoes in this field or that, and who slept where?

We didn't see as much of Pa and when we did it was flying visits, often accompanied by men we didn't know. There was a great increase in traffic on the distant roads. We started to see army and air force people with Pa. They were commandeering vast areas of the countryside to build airfields and camps. We knew then that no matter what the politicians said we would soon be at war.

I had forgotten to get the accumulator recharged, so we sat with our ears close to the wireless, straining, trying to catch every fading word that Mr Chamberlain spoke that Sunday morning. The waiting was over, we were at war.

Phyllis got her wish; we became respectable, we got curtains, albeit blackout ones. Pa advised us to rent more land, as much as we could, he said, and we did.

We dried, bottled, salted and jammed everything that came out of the land, dykes, and hedgerows. I had even managed to kill a chicken with my eyes open. We hid our food in buildings, in trees and in the land, determined that the enemy would not profit from our hard work if we were invaded.

One huge change in our life was the flood of noise that washed over us. Wind, bird, the cry of a fox and the gentle sounds of our own animals had been our only companions. Now the boom of the bittern was lost in the sound of the bomber, the nightingale's song was drowned in the roar of fighter planes.

It was the late summer of 1940. The war wasn't going well. Our forces were in retreat everywhere and the country tense waiting for invasion. Phyllis heard it first. We lifted our heads from the row of cabbages and scanned all the paths and dykes. There it was, edging along a narrow path between the dykes. A motorbike with two men on it. They edged nearer and we could see the dark leather coats, boots and close fitting helmets.

Germans, breathed Phyllis. We lay flat, hidden between the cabbage stalks, peering, praying, and trying not to breathe.

They stopped at the door. The pillion passenger got off, he strode forward, his leather coat long and foreign. He knocked. They listened to the silence, then he hammered on the door. Phyllis bristled. I grabbed her arm and held it tight. He stood legs apart, tall, arrogant, looking around with interest, then slowly sauntered to the barn as if he owned the place. He pulled the door open and just walked in.

This was too much, German or no German. We had a flitch of bacon hanging in there and no German was getting his hands on that. We jumped up, yelling and screaming at the top of our voices. Phyllis was clutching a rake in one hand and a spade in the other. We were both streaked with sweat and soil. I don't know who was the most surprised, the man who ran, open mouthed out of the barn, the one struggling to keep his motorbike upright, or us, at the amount of noise we had created.

Come out, you thieving Germans, Phyllis screamed.

I was so angry I can't remember all that came out of my mouth. I didn't realise I knew, never mind had the nerve to use such ripe language.

The two men stood motionless, staring at us, eyes startled, mouths open. They seemed to grow taller, more menacing. I started to feel uneasy. I could feel the hair on my neck starting to stand up. The taller man's face started to redden. I felt my chest tighten. He threw his head back and peals of laughter rolled over us. He spoke to his companion in some incomprehensible language, the shouts of laughter started again from both of them. It was our turn to stare. They straightened, the taller one managed to control his laughter, and his face went serious.

You insult us.

He saluted, clicked his heels and said.

I will introduce ourselves to you, we are Aleksander Baranowski and Jozef Jablonski of the Polish Free Air force.

With big smiles they thrust their hands towards us. It was to be the start of a wonderful friendship.

The Meeting House

In the first months of the war I received cajoling letters from my mother asking me to go home. The reasons she gave were various. The first one being that I was nearer to Germany than she was and would be murdered in my bed if we were invaded. The next, a woman living alone is vulnerable. I pointed out that I didn't live alone, that Phyllis shared the house with me. Twice a week such letters would arrive. Once a week I would reply, either ignoring or refusing the offer of a place back in the nest. Then I made the mistake of writing about the two Polish airmen. I received dire warnings on being friendly with foreigners. At last, even my mother realised that I was not going to leave my beloved cottage.

We saw the lads or old boys as Phyllis called them, often. Sometimes it would be just the one, but usually we would hear the motorbike and the next moment we would be hugged and made a fuss of by them both. They obviously had a good friend in the cookhouse, or they were adept at acquiring goods. They would carefully ease a few envelopes out of their pockets like magicians. A few ounces of sugar, half a dozen teaspoons of tea, the same of coffee which they swore they had seen being made from acorns. As far as Phyllis was concerned the pinnacle was reached when a bar of chocolate appeared. It was part of their airborne rations designed to give them quick energy on those long stressful flights. Aleksander who spoke good English maintained that it was to offer to the natives if they were shot down. Often it wasn't a full bar or even half a bar. It become a ritual, a piece of chocolate became a good luck omen to them. On every flight they saved at least one square for Phyllis. They felt it ensured that they would get home safely. It seemed that every member of an aircrew had a superstition or special routine that they wouldn't alter or break no matter what. Theirs was the piece of chocolate for Phyllis.

Full of curiosity, we asked why they had first knocked at our door. They both grinned, Aleksander explained.

Jozef's family have, or should I say had, large landholdings near the Russian border. That is before Russia joined Germany in occupying Poland. He insisted that this land looked identical to his. He longed to walk on it and

25

feel the soil. We smiled and nodded our heads. We could understand that.

Then we argued whether this building was a ruin or a shack, so we came to see.

We both bristled at the thought that our home could be mistaken for a shack. Which amused them.

Over the next few visits it was obvious that Jozef longed to touch and work the land. It wasn't long before he would greet us, disappear into the barn and emerge in old rag-and-tag clothing and within seconds he'd be digging, ditching, weeding, planting, clearing, and doing all the tasks that made up farming. He soon found an ancient plough in the barn and spent hours repairing, cleaning and getting it in good order.

Then Pa was set the job of finding a horse. It had to be strong, trained to the plough and cheap. We should have added 'and not heading for the knackers yard'.

Of course it was no sooner said than done with Pa. The horse arrived, and Phyllis and I unwittingly provided great entertainment as we attempted to put a collar and what seemed like a hundred leather straps on to the poor nag. Then we had to attempt hitching the plough. Those two boys came close to being banned forever from our home.

Aleksander added to our mortification by sketching the whole proceedings on a carefully hoarded sheet of brown paper. A mathematician, turned by the war into a navigator, he had a compulsion to sketch. Two or three rapid lines on the small pad he always carried and the essence of a bird, flower or animal was caught.

The pair would be absent for some weeks and of an evening we would watch the planes as they flew out in dark, droning, formation. They never returned in formation. We would count them out and try to count them back home, but it was impossible. There were always those who came coughing, spluttering, looking like sieves, hours after the main group straggled in. Often, we could see the gaping holes where panels had been shot or burnt away. We couldn't speak, were often in tears as we prayed to every God we had heard of to get them home safely.

When the boys came back from operations they looked terrible. Haggard, grey, tired, sometimes angry, often depressed, and frightened. They were so different. Phyllis would be given a dozen or so squares of chocolate which for some reason known only to herself she kept in an egg box. Then the boys would start what I always thought of as their healing routine. Aleksander would go to the path that he was making, that came from nowhere and was going nowhere. The earth was dug, piled up, and then flattened with mighty strikes from the back of the spade. This would continue for half an hour or so, then he would just sit looking at it, slowly drawing on a cigarette. Jozef would get the big saw and attack logs at breakneck speed. They would be thrown with all his might at the woodpile. Some time much later they would be stacked neatly. When everything had been sawn and struck out of them, they would amble into the barn, lie on some straw and sleep like babies for a few hours.

Only rarely would they mention companions who were missing. More often they spoke of their families. Aleksander would worry about his wife and two children. We knew all about them and had seen their photographs so often that Phyllis swore that we would recognise them if we saw them in the street. Jozef was convinced that he would never see his family again and said all he wanted was to survive the war, then he would plan his life.

Phyllis and I were on the go from daybreak to darkness and beyond. We bartered, trying to add a bit of variety to our meagre rations. Three fresh eggs for a pound of sugar, a chicken for a packet of tea or anything else we needed. We found an old butter churn in the barn and after trial and error we started to produce an edible butter. We were getting good milk from the cow, so the next task to master was cheese making. We didn't know a cheese maker, even Pa drew a blank. All dead and gone, he reckoned. We were desolate. We had visions of cartwheels of cheese maturing in the barn, cheese and home made bread, cheese on toast for supper in front of the fire every winter's night, and enough left over for a little bartering.

Once again Phyllis and Pa were our saviours. They knew of the local custom passed down and added to by each generation; the Family Book. A lot of generations had written down their special recipes for food, cleaners, polishes, soaps, their home made cures for both man and beast, their fertiliser, sheep dip and home brew. Within a week we had dozens of recipes. Cheese making became an absorbing challenge and we relished it. I learned so much about so many skills from those old notebooks. We even started our own book in a great fat ledger that Pa donated.

On rare, quiet occasions I would wonder about the families who had lived in the cottage before us. Had they kept a family book? I didn't doubt that they had made cheese, butter and all the things that we were trying to do. But how had they survived war, poverty and want? What had driven him to hang himself?

In our first weeks here, we did what Phyllis assured me everyone who lived in isolated places did. We bought a tin trunk from the salesroom, painted our names on it and placed it where the path finally met the road. The postman would leave our post in it, at the same time collecting any letters we were sending, also any shopping lists or messages. The little Post Office was like a clearing station, strictly unofficial but it kept the community together. The carrier did the same when he passed. He would take to the Post Office any letters and messages and shopping lists to the relevant shop. He would then get the job of delivering the completed order back to us. Since the start of the war we had received a lot more mail, mostly in brown envelopes from the Ministry of Food or Agriculture, but we were astounded one day to receive one from the Ministry of War. We spent a few minutes turning it over and over making outlandish guesses about its contents, none of which matched the surprise we got on opening it. There was a lot of flannelling about the great part agriculture was doing to help the war effort, then came the shock, the knockout:

We wish to inform you that two German prisoners of war will be working unaccompanied in the area around your land. They will be clearing dykes and ditches between 8am and 5am five days per week. They are not considered to be a threat to safety.

Well this was definitely something not to tell my Mother.

Within a few weeks they were working on our dykes. In brown battle dress with large brightly coloured diamonds and triangles on the front and back of every piece of uniform, they were easily seen. We wondered what they were thinking as they shaded their eyes and watched the planes returning from bombing raids. We watched them and they watched us. We started to lock the door when we worked in the fields. The boys locked their motorbike in the barn and carried the ignition key with them. When all was said and done they were the enemy and not to be trusted.

Jozef and Alaksander made the first contact with them. They were young, inquisitive and could speak a little German. They also realised that most people were given no choice about being involved in a war.

Life wasn't all hard work. We loved listening to the wireless. We laughed with ITMA and were terrified by The Man In Black, and like the rest of the country everything stopped for the news bulletins at night. My father on his first visit had brought a gramophone and a wide selection of records. 'The Ink Spots' lulled us with 'If I didn't care'. The Andrew Sisters drove me mad singing 'The woodpeckers song'. Phyllis loved it. 'The three records of Chopin were special to me. We pushed the furniture back and with Victor Sylvester taught Phyllis ballroom dancing. We let her down badly though. She longed to learn the tango and the rumba after seeing a Carmen Miranda film. Alas not one of us had ever attempted it. Jozef's offer to teach her the Polish Polka was no compensation, but he still taught it. We knitted socks, hats, gloves, for soldiers and sailors and blankets for the bombed out. We sat snug in winter listening to and singing our version of opera, ballads and popular songs.

There was one record that caught the essence of this land and the wide, changing, wonderful skies above it. When Jozef heard The Lark Ascending he was transfixed. He became obsessed with the music. It was played every time he came, tears would hover in his eyes as he sat listening. It is the sound of my home, he would say.

Jozef could play the flute and was determined to find one. He scoured music shops and pawnshops but it was Pa who weeks later found one and a box of manuscripts including 'The Lark in the clear air' and an arrangement almost complete for the flute. Finishing the arrangement became Jozef's new healing routine.

The flute became our friend's constant companion, He would sit in a field listening to a skylark and then we would hear the haunting answering flute. We were amused when his flute was banished from the camp after he was found playing in the ablution block at two in the morning. Our mantle shelf became its resting-place.

The POWs worked steadily around us, they became part of our day and slowly we relaxed. They would join us for a mug of tea at midday and before long we were once again listening to the fears of men parted from their families. Ernst and Hans were delighted to be prisoners, reasoning that they were safe and the Eastern Front was someone else's nightmare. It was like a club, the four men would have a game of cards, or chess, other times a quiet easy conversation and perhaps the wireless or a record played, then it was back to the grindstone for us all.

It was a noisy, scurrying, windy day and our heads were down as we weeded the onion patch. Neither of us had heard a motorbike coming along the track. It just seemed to arrive. We screwed up our eyes trying to block the dust and peer at the stranger. I heard Phyllis gasp,

Oh no.

What was wrong with the girl, what did she mean, oh no?

Then I knew. I felt sick, I couldn't speak, my heart contracted and even the wind seemed to hold its breath.

The officer walked towards us and we turned and clung to each other.

There was no easy way for him to tell us but he tried. Slowly and gently he tried to pierce our numbness and we stood staring at him, his words part of the shock and the horror.

A night raid .... badly damaged .... Jozef with great skill got it back to England .... Shot to pieces .... crash landing in Kent .... Aleksander dead .... everyone but Jozef dead .... very badly burned and in hospital.

We didn't notice him go, he just faded from our consciousness. We sat on the ground shivering, holding each other. Ernst and Hans found us. They had seen the officer and knew from experience what his message had been. They held our hands as the grieving tears and sobs broke.

The International House

The writing on this envelope was different. It looked masculine. Thick, heavy, with golf ball full stops. There was a group of volunteers who went in to the hospital to write the men's letters but we didn't recognise this one. We were pleased when a woman wrote. They would often add a scrap of paper with a comment or two about Jozef. There was more news in those couple of lines than in a page full of his dictated letter. We had developed a routine with his letters, who ever collected them from the old tin trunk that was our post box, read them to the other. So we sat together on a bale of straw in the barn and Phyllis started to read the letter, but it wasn't from Jozef. She hesitated, glanced at the signature and her startled eyes swivelled to my face. We both caught our breath.

It's from a doctor.

Oh no.

Phyllis devoured the letter, then a smile lit her face, her eyes danced.

Anything but. They want to know if we would like to go to visit for a weekend and there is accommodation we can book in the grounds of the hospital.

We hugged each other, laughing and crying. We thought this day would never come.

The winter day seemed brighter, the anaemic sun warmer. Oh yes, the. tide of war had turned, just as Mr Churchill had said.

Jozef and Aleksander had been our friends since the early days of the war. Polish airmen in exile was how they described themselves, They yearned for their families and their homes. I'm not quite sure who adopted whom but they spent most of their time between flying operations here. They had been like dearly loved brothers to us. They flew together and were injured together. Aleksander died of his injuries and Jozef lived but was badly burned. He had been in a specialist hospital for six months having skin grafts. We had never heard of skin grafts, and to be truthful I don't think my father, who was a doctor knew much about them. He certainly made it his business to find out and keep us informed. I still find the procedure unbelievable. The hospital authorities banned visiting and said that they would inform us when we could visit. We didn't imagine that it would be half a year!

There was so much to decide, so much to plan As we explained to Hans and Ernst our German friends only one of us could go. We had the animals to care for, but we both wanted to go and we were both invited. Within two minutes Ernst had a solution mapped out. Ask Phyllis's Pa to take charge for a few days. Before that write to the Commander of the P.O.W. camp explaining the situation and asking if they, Hans and Ernst, could help on the farm for a few days. It seemed so easy when he suggested it. None of us had experienced British army bureaucracy. They checked with the Police that we were patriotic citizens, that we didn't have a boat or large amounts of money. They sent an officer to check on the situation of the cottage. The fact that it took him two and a half-hours to find us should have said it all. A few days later they gave their agreement.

It took us twenty-three hours travelling to get to the hospital. The train was crammed with people. Soldiers sleeping in corridors sprawled on kit bags, reading, playing cards. Sailors snoozing in luggage racks, others stood any where that they could plant their two feet. Windows streamed with condensation, and cigarette smoke. We were shunted into sidings, held at signals, stopped at stations while troop trains, ammunition, or as the soldiers maintained, generals and top brass speeded through. We had been warned to take something to eat and drink and we needed it. Because of spies the name of every station had been obliterated. We had no idea where we were. Luckily the guard had been brought out of retirement and knew the line well. He scrambled over bodies and luggage to warn us that the next stop was ours and hoped that we would have good news!

Although the staff had prepared us, we were apprehensive as we walked towards the ward accompanied by a nurse who looked and walked like a film star. We heard laughter and the click of billiard balls. The first thing we saw from the doorway was a barrel of beer, there it sat on trestles in the front of the ward. We looked at each other, what kind of hospital was this? We took one step through the door and wished the floor would open up and swallow us. Wolf whistles came from every side and kept on coming, requests to go to a dance, a walk, the pictures or a pub followed. We just had to laugh. After a greeting like that, it was impossible to stare in horror or to recoil from these young men and their terrible injuries. The banter between them and the nurse was like listening to a game of verbal tennis!

We knew it was Jozef, even though it wasn't Jozef's face. There were still traces of his distinctive walk in the slow, awkward gait of the man coming towards us. Phyllis ran and put her arms around him hugging him tight. There was a chorus of cheers, whistles and shouts of, My turn now, share it.

Then as Phyllis stepped back she was swung around and waltzed all over the floor by a stranger, his head bandaged to the size of the Town Hall clock. The accompanying cheers and claps brought the house down and half a dozen young men waiting their turn!

It gave me a few seconds to steal a glance at Jozef. His face red, the skin twisted and torturous, eyelids dragged down, the front of his head hairless, his ears virtually nonexistent and his neck swathed in bandages. He raised his arms towards me and I saw his hands. I knew then that I would be taking his flute home with me.

We were exhausted, and felt as if we had been through an emotional mangle when we arrived home at last. Pa, Ernst and Hans listened, silent and distressed as we recounted what we had seen. Phyllis and I could hold back the tears no longer and sobbed ourselves empty. Yet there was work to be done. Jozef was coming. A six months gap in his treatment meant that he would be sent to a convalescent home. We knew he would sooner be with us, walking the land, watching the clouds in our great open sky. Why is it, we only think of the practicalities later? Sleeping space, emergencies and if we were capable of coping with Jozef, his injuries and changes that we couldn't even begin to imagine. Nothing that can't be solved was Pa's philosophy, which he demonstrated a week or so later when we watched a farm tractor slowly towing a small dilapidated caravan along the track. Only used at lambing time, it had stood in the corner of a field until Pa pointed out to the farmer how it could be used to help the war effort. We were like children playing with a doll's house. Scrubbing, polishing, trying to get rid of the smell of sheep, which defied all our efforts.

Life was certainly a challenge once Jozef arrived. It took a few weeks before we could accept that if he wanted help, he would ask for it. He had many of what we came to call 'black dog days' Days when we would catch a glimpse of him in the distance walking the banks of the dykes. He would be out all day and we would try to track him with our eyes as we worked, uneasy and protective towards him. As the weeks and months progressed these days became less. We even got used to the sound of a tool or bucket hitting the barn wall as he vented his frustration.

Hans and Ernst by gentle persuasion and our entreaties had convinced the camp commander that they would be more use with us, than clearing ditches. They became great friends of Jozef's and were his anchor. Ernst was one of those men who could see a problem and work out a practical solution to it. Gadgets started to appear, something added here to an everyday item, something taken away there, an angle added to a fork, a wide rubber band that fixed a spoon in his hand, a contraption that enabled Jozef to cut bread, peel potatoes.

There was one happening that we had no control over, it always affected Jozef, always led him to start walking. America was now in the war and had massive airfields in the area, that sent massive numbers, of massive bombers on day and night raids over Germany. He would watch them fly out and wait for them to come back. He seemed to have a sixth sense about the time of their return and would stand in the early hours outside the caravan just scanning the heavens. It was the ones that came late, sometimes two or three hours later that would start him walking. There was a popular song at that time Coming in on a wing and a prayer. Jozef's prayers bombarded heaven, asking for the crew's safe landing. If he judged that they wouldn't make it to base he would start walking, always in the direction they had flown. Why? I always felt it was part of him coping, trying to prevent his injuries being repeated.

The plane had come in low, virtually clipping the tops of the trees We could see the pilot.

He's not going to make it! was shouted and Jozef was gone, with Hans and Ernst following.

Phyllis and I watched the plane labouring, spluttering and struggling lower and lower. We willed it along, we prayed it would get back safe and every one in it. Ernst and Hans came back two hours later, but no Jozef.

We watched the clock, we walked toward the horizon hoping to see a speck coming towards us, nothing. Seven hours later we saw a speck. Moving rapidly, faster than a man could walk or run and coming here. We thought the worst.

We watched the jeep pull up and we gasped as we saw this giant unwind out of it.

Colonel John O'Malley the third. I have a gentleman who says he lives here, he said.

We got a second shock as a Negro got out of the driving seat, reached into the back and gently lifted the sleeping Jozef out as if he was a child.

Neither Phyllis nor myself had ever seen a Negro before, then realised how rude we were staring at him with our mouths open. We led them into the cottage, both had to stoop to go through the door.

The sleeping Jozef was laid so gently on the sofa.

Do you actually live here, asked the Colonel.

I don't know whether he asked in amazement or disbelief as his eyes swept the room.

Yes, I barked.

He flushed, it was his turn to be embarrassed. He shook his head and smiled the most wonderful smile and started to tell his and Jozef's tale. How they had arrived at the crashed plane at virtually the same time. How the plane was alight and ammunition exploding in all directions. Jozef trying to reach the crew and his terrible distress when he couldn't and realised that there was nothing that could be done to help them. The Colonel couldn't understand what Jozef was saying but realised that he had faced the same situation. He had given him a sedative after finding out where he lived and here they were.

He wanted to know all about Jozef. It was obvious from his questions that he was a doctor and we told him everything. We offered him a cup of tea and it was apparent from the downward turn of his mouth what he thought of tea. So a glass of home brew was offered and accepted. He frowned when we poured the beer and handed it to the men. The Colonel's face was stony, the other man didn't lift his eyes from the floor. Had we upset them? There was something. Something had passed between these two men which I couldn't interpret. Before long I could, quite easily.

The Troubled House

I think one of us should train as a nurse. A mental nurse. Phyllis waited for my response.

She has a point, I thought. Jozef had been recalled to hospital under the guise of starting preparations for his next series of grafts. In truth it was to treat the profound depression that had smothered him following that plane crash. We had made the long journey once again to see him. We told him that the caravan was always there for him and that we wanted him back. There was no response from him, no smile, no hug, no words. It was impossible to pierce the blackness around him. Months later we were still racked with the thought that had we known more about his condition the more we may have been able to help him.

Then the letter arrived that led to Phyllis's comment. There was another airman, thousands of miles from home, a country boy, friend of Jozef, who also had a six months break in his treatment. He persuaded his scribe to write a pleading letter to us, asking if we would be willing to give him a home for that length of time? She added a note which was full of affection for him.

Of course we will, was Phyllis's reaction. I was more hesitant, still raw, still shocked by the changes in our friend. We discussed it with Hans and Ernst, who had been so closely involved with Jozef. We agreed that it was a responsibility and that the last months with Jozef had drained us all. They were both silent, deep in thought. Then Hans lifted his head.

Come on spit it out, Hans, I said.

He looked at me blankly.

Tell us what's on your mind.

He swallowed and his blue eyes held my face.

Working here, accepted by people I consider to be my friends, who do not blame me, personally, for the war, has enabled me to accept and cope with being a P.O.W. I will in time go home and pick up the threads of my old life. These young men have terrible injuries that many people will turn away from. Their lives will never be the same and the sooner they learn to cope with the stares and what life has to throw at them the better. We can help them in that.

I stared at my hands, ashamed that I had hesitated.

Jonty Pilkington, aged 23 years, citizen of Australia, a rear gunner with terrible disfiguring burns arrived and gave our lives a shaking that they never recovered from. The first person he saw was Phyllis. He marched up to her and said,

G'day don't you recognise me?

She stared at him and shook her head.

I'm the bloke who danced with you when you came to the hospital.

She smiled. Seeing that your head and face was bandaged and all I could see were your eyes, I've more chance of recognising your bandages than you.

He threw back his head as far as the scar tissue on his neck would allow and let out a peal of laughter. It was a foretaste of our life to come. They teased and tormented each other mercilessly. Wherever Jonty went, chuckles and laughter followed.

Hans and Ernst were intrigued by this thin, small man. A farmer's son, who would tackle anything but had a special affinity with animals. He would talk and sing to them, usually Australian rugby songs, which he reckoned were more interesting and filthy than English ones. It wasn't long before they were being sung with German accents. Pa dubbed them the Three Musketeers.

Jonty and Pa would have long discussions on farm management and before long was accompanying Pa on his visits. Jonty's home farm in Australia had thousands of acres of land. Soon virtually every farmer in the county knew about this Down Under farm and the invitations soon flowed asking him to give talks about it. It was like a fairy story to them. Thousands of acres and some of them had twenty! The home brew flowed freely and at the end of the night Jonty would be deposited at our door, singing at the top of his voice and accompanied by as many farmers sober enough to fit on a tractor, wagon, boat and on one occasion a horse that brought him home.

Our nearest town was little more than a large village, yet to him it was paradise. Pubs, church dances, beetle drives, the local choir, dramatics, he attended them all. He even offered his services to the tiny Salvation Army band, which they were reluctantly forced to refuse. As he himself admitted, his musical instrument was the mouth organ and he played that badly! One of the farmers, who became a great pal, gave Jonty a great heavy boneshaker of a bike. He maintained it was the best physiotherapy he had ever had. Before long he had persuaded Phyllis to go with him to dances, organ recitals or anything else that was going on. A cushion was tied tightly to the crossbar and with much laughter Phyllis would perch on to it, then off they set to ride the five miles to town. I told them that they were mad.

Colonel O'Malley developed the habit of dropping in on odd occasions. He seemed to overwhelm and fill our cottage, there was so much of him. He always came by jeep, always driven by the same Negro, the one who had carried Jozef in so gently. It was after a few visits that we realised that he never followed Colonel O'Malley indoors. It was Jonty, on a day when the wind and rain swept through the open sided jeep who found the reason why. He shouted from the door of the caravan for the serviceman to go in and shelter. He refused. Jonty said he could actually hear the chatter of his teeth and his bones playing the Hallelujah chorus as he shivered. Intrigued, Jonty dashed to the jeep, dived in and told the man to drive it into the barn. He wrapped a threadbare horse blanket and a couple of sacks around the man and packed his feet in straw. He told him he was a fool to sit out in this kind of weather. Jonty was stopped in mid-sentence when the soldier said he had only been obeying orders. Few of Jonty's question were answered. The only information that he gave easily was his name, Abel, and that he came from Alabama. Yes Sir, No Sir was the stock reply to Jonty's questions about living in England, the weather, America, or the war. Jonty said that it was like trying to milk a gnat.

A one-sided conversation is frustrating and Jonty was fast losing interest. He idly fished his mouth organ out of his breast pocket and it was as if he had switched on a light. Their conversation flew along and in a very short space of time the mouth organ was singing as it had never done before. Abel from Alabama, as Jonty called him, was a virtuoso.

It was a lovely period in our lives. The war was going well, the wet, cold winter was forgotten, spring had been all that it should be and the summer was glorious.

Jozef was back with us, quiet, but not withdrawn and more at ease with himself. Sharing a caravan with Jonty was good therapy.

A couple of evenings a week Abel and four or five of his friends would get dropped off the recreation truck as it passed the end of the track and then the bone- shaker would be used to ferry them down to the cottage.

Often we would sit outside enjoying the evening sun just talking and listening to them talk about their homes. Our idea of America was pure Hollywood and we were appalled as slowly, a picture of their lives emerged. It explained Colonel O'Malley's attitude towards Negroes. Then there were those special evenings, the ones memories are made of. The ones when mouth organs, upturned barrels and paper and combs were played, When the birds sang their hearts out in competition. Yet there was a quietness, a peace as they merged. Often when they were homesick, Spirituals would be softly played and sung. After all these years I still want to cry when I hear one. Other times it would be far livelier, the music tumbling along often accompanied by a tap dance or their strange shuffling dance. Then they made the mistake of telling Phyllis about this new dance, called jive or jitterbug. She was determined that they would teach her it and teach it now. And that was the cause of the trouble.

It started innocently enough, a thoughtless question, and an answer acted on by a man we later considered to be a jealous, arrogant man

The question was to Abel, called by Phyllis as he drove the Colonel away from the cottage.

You are coming tonight to teach me the jitterbug?

A hand was raised in the affirmative. The Colonel's face was tight and closed.

He didn't like that, or the thoughts of you flinging your body around with a Negro said Jonty.

It's our home and we've invited them. He can't do anything about it was Phyllis' reply.

Oh, how mistaken we were.

Phyllis was one of those people with a great sense of rhythm and quick to learn. Isaac was beating out In the Mood on the doorstep with a metal spike, the rest of us, in-between laughing at Abel and Phyllis' contortions, were trying to sing at something like the speed of the beat and failing miserably. Jonty saw them first and with that strange telepathy that a group of friends have, we were all soon staring along the track.

Man, this is trouble, big trouble said Isaac in what was almost a whisper.

Don't talk daft. You're our friends and invited to be here, I said.

Where we all come from, there ain't no such a thing as friendship between Negroes and White people, especially female ones, said Isaac.

39

Jozef and Jonty walked to the start of the track, forcing the jeeps to stop. Of the four men in them, three got out leaving the driver revving his engine loudly. It sounded so threatening. Then we saw the truncheons they held at their sides.

Jozef walked toward the jeep and we could see the shock when the driver looked into his face. Jozef spoke and the jeep went still. We had thought Colonel O' Malley gigantic, but he was nothing compared with these men. The largest and most bedecked with badges, stepped forward and introduced himself and then turned towards Abel.

You niggers ain't got no right here.

These men are our friends. They are invited here and surely should be addressed as Soldier. Jonty's voice was cold and polite.

The man froze. These nigger soldiers are not allowed to visit or consort with decent white women, He slowly moved his head and let his eyes lazily slide over Phyllis from her neck to her toes.

The niggers are coming with us. And that is an order.

Jonty took a step forward. Immediately they tightened their grip on the truncheons.

Abel spoke. Jonty, we're going. You'll only make it worse.

Our friends reluctantly walked towards the jeeps. Abel went sprawling on the floor as a foot was stuck in front of him. A truncheon was jabbed into his kidneys, a heavy booted foot stepped on to his arm, he cried out and was hauled to his feet and flung into a jeep. As the others made their way, truncheons managed to find knees, elbows, fingers and backs before they were manhandled into the jeeps.

Both Jozef and Jonty shouted and started to move forward. The men spun around, their whole stance just daring them to continue. The Americans slowly climbed into their vehicles, revved and revved the engines and then were gone.

We stood in a group, shocked, angry. We couldn't understand what had happened and why. Then human nature being what it is, we started to relive the last week looking for a reason, an explanation. It didn't take long before we were convinced that Colonel O'Malley had been the person to set it all in motion. We knew that we had to protest.

We sent two letters, one informing the Colonel that he was no longer welcome at our home and the reasons why. We received no reply. The second we sent to the commanding officer of the American base, explaining and complaining about the treatment of our friends. A month later we received a reply stating that after an investigation, it was judged that our complaint was without foundation, and adding that the soldiers were no longer at that base.

The Changing House

The war was drawing to a close and in the house a romance was opening. Phyllis and Jonty, had been good friends since the first day he arrived. She appeared to treat him as a brother, but it was different with Jonty. He always seemed to be aware of her, where she was and what she was doing. It was years later that Jozef mentioned Jonty's determination to marry Phyllis since their first hospital meeting. I think Phyllis became aware of him as someone other than a brother when they started their trips together on the boneshaker. The changes were subtle, the special glances, the searching eyes when one of them left or entered a room, a touch, a soft word, their bodies just that tiny bit closer to each other. We all watched over the romance like a clutch of mother hens. It made us feel good, every day had pleasure and warmth in it. Pa didn't hesitate when Jonty asked his permission to marry Phyllis.

It was to be a quiet wedding. Then the news spread. Every farmer Jonty knew, and there were a great many, offered chickens, a ham, butter, or game. Their wives offered to make brawn, bake, make a special home brew and trifles. Rationing was forgotten. Every society or choir that Jonty had joined collected food or clothing coupons. People offered to lend bridal and bridesmaids' dresses, some were forty, fifty, years old. One had never been worn, the prospective groom having been killed in the first war. It was growing into anything but a quiet wedding. Once that became obvious, it was thrown open to everyone.

They came from miles around and in country fashion all brought something for the feast. The tables were stacked high with food, but the bottles and barrels of home brew were stacked even higher. Jonty and Jozef were in uniform, Hans and Ernst by special dispensation were allowed to wear civvies for a day (Pa borrowed them from a man who knew a man who knew a man).

The sky was a never-ending blue canvas and Phyllis looked breathtaking.

The only change that the marriage brought to our lives was that the happy couple moved into my bedroom and I moved into Phyllis's. We cared for the land, the animals and each other as we always had. Life seemed full of hope.

The war ended about six months later. We heard the announcement on the wireless, just as we had heard the beginning, it was just a different Prime Minister.

Jonty, all treatments finished, sailed for home a few months later, with Phyllis to follow. Every day she cycled up the track checking for letters, even though we told her the ship had hardly set sail, never mind reached Cape Town and it would be many weeks before it would reach Australia. It brought back all those terrible months when we had waited for letters from Jozef.

Then the news I dreaded arrived; Phyllis was given a sailing date. She was on cloud nine at first, but as the day came nearer she grew more and more anxious. Would his parents like her, would she cope with the heat? She spent the best part of one day wondering if she could live without rain. Can you imagine that! At last the day arrived. We clung to each other sobbing, promising to write and keep in touch. We meant so much to each other. Jozef was made to promise to look after me, I was made to promise to look after Jozef and her Pa, and then she was gone. No matter where we turned or what we did we missed her, and the hole that she left in our lives has never been filled.

Hans and Ernst were with us for another year. Ernst, married with children, longed to go home. When he did, he found his home destroyed and his family scattered. He would send the occasional letter and Christmas card. Then ten years later a letter came saying that he would be in England with his new wife and could he call?

He was still the same Ernst, just a stone heavier, ten years older and prosperous. He had never found his wife and children and after six years of searching had been granted a divorce. Two years later he had met and married Anna. We asked if he knew anything at all about Hans. Their early letters to me had been full of their meetings. Then, as with us, the letters and Christmas cards from Hans had stopped. Ernst explained that it had become more and more difficult for Hans to visit West Germany or for him to go into the East. It was impossible to get a pass for the Russian sector, which was now isolated by the Berlin wall. The last time they'd met, Hans had been very agitated about the curtailment of civic freedoms in the East. It was following that meeting that the letters stopped. Ernst was convinced that Hans was either in prison, shipped to Russia, or dead.

Anna was lovely, blonde, pretty and very down to earth. When she arrived, she stood so still and quiet just staring at the sky. It seems that she had promised Ernst that she would do this. As she said, he compared every sky he saw to the high, vast, wonderful skies in England. I was intrigued and asked if she liked them.

No, was the answer, I feel naked under them.

I liked her a lot.

The war had been over some years, when one early spring morning instead of leaving our letters in the old tin trunk, Harry Sneddle drew up in his red van. Our post was always very mundane, Harry was a notorious gossip, so I knew there was something unusual in his bag. With a cup of tea and a couple of slices of toast he was obviously settled for half an hour. He always enjoyed spinning out the suspense but this time it was obvious that his inquisitiveness was ready to burst out. He studied a long white envelope, handed it to me and asked if it could be intended for me. I glanced at it and understand why he was asking. There was my Christian name. Below that was written:

The lonely little cottage between the streams.
About 4-5miles east of Fenton
East Anglia

I stared at it, turned it over. I didn't recognise the writing.

Well, I could open it and put 'opened in error' if it's not for me. With that I tore it open.

I read it, read it again, then sat down in shock. I could read Harry's expression. He knew that here was a choice bit of gossip that would interest every house on his round. It crossed my mind that he'd stop at every address today, whether he had post for them or not. Then he would regale everyone back at the post office. The whole town would know by tomorrow. Oh what did it matter. They'd be so happy passing it around. Although I did wonder if the final story would resemble the truth.

He sat, barely able to control his curiosity.

It's from an American we haven't heard from since the end of the war. He was a great friend of Jonty. He may be coming to see us in the next few months

How his nose quivered. Being well mannered, he couldn't ask for more details even though he longed to. He stood up, no time to stop, urgent deliveries, which was true. The delivery of gossip is always urgent. He couldn't wait to get the drums rolling. When he was gone, I read the letter again.

Abel had survived the war and returning to America took stock of his life. He decided to live in the North and to get an education. He could barely read or write at the start of the war. There was a small amount of help offered by the U.S. Government, but to pay his way and survive, he had got a job as a singer with a dance band. It had been hard, singing until four in a morning and then classes during the day. He graduated and became a schoolteacher in what he called a ghetto. His love of music was still a driving force in his life and he had trained a school choir and what he called a blow and strum band He was hoping to bring them to England for a prestigious competition. Unfortunately, over the next few months, it became clear that very poor pupils from a very poor school couldn't even raise a quarter of the money needed for the trip.

But we had made contact. It was in the third letter that I found out what a blow and strum band was. What a good name for a mouth organ and banjo band. I couldn't imagine what they would sound like!

Then Frances, you arrived out of the blue. I still can't believe it. Before you were born, your Mum wrote and said that she was expecting and if the baby was a girl, she would like to call her Frances after me. I was so happy. That was a long time ago. I've watched you growing up long distance, if you understand what I mean. Photographs, letters and then that trip when you were eighteen. Your Grandpa talked about it for years. I loved the three months that you were here. Jonty was right when he told you just to come. Our big, peaceful, summer skies, are great healers. They make you realise that you are just one tiny stitch in life's tapestry. You seemed more content, happier, when you left for home. Oh, didn't we do some talking? All about the house and its people. What memories were stirred. It was a shock to realise that some were still painful. I think it is a lovely idea to write a history of the house for your parents, and as you say, with your contacts you may even get it published. I can't imagine a book about our shabby, dear old house. I keep scribbling down incidents and memories I have of those special early days. Even Josef has started a book, written in Polish of course. Jonty figures strongly in them. Josef has always considered your father as his saviour. I'm told it is a sign of ageing when you start to live in the past. I think we both must be ancient.

Such a small isolated house. Such a wealth of experiences and memories. Such lives.

The Waiting House

I've studied the past so often, recalled friends, my cottage, the lives lived in it and I completely ignore that life is still being lived under its roof. I did promise to continue what Frances called 'The Cottage Chronicles' but three years have slipped by without me gathering my thoughts and memories.

No, that's not true, they are always with me, it's writing them down where I'm remiss. I suppose the last few years have belonged to Jozef. It's not that he demands my time, more that I feel the need to give him my time. He has borne so many of life's crosses. The older he gets the more cantankerous he gets. There is no happy medium, he's either up or down. He went through every known channel trying to trace his family after the war. He had always maintained that the Russians would kill them and they did, every single one of them. After the war his home and family estates were confiscated by the Communists and given to a party minister. Jozef will never go back to Poland, most of his life has been spent here where he feels secure. As he has aged, the scar tissue, especially on his face has altered. People find it hard to look at him and never meet his eyes. He heard a young woman remark, that if she looked like him she would kill herself. Her friends laughed. It makes me so angry and sad when I think of his life and all that he lost for this country.

Jozef bought a larger caravan and refused to get rid of the old one. It's held together with bits and pieces of wood, string, rope, and a metal sign advertising Oxydol that he found in a hedge. It's the centre of his latest battle with the Council, one of many. I keep telling him that he'll wear the old typewriter out with his letters. The Council say it's an eyesore and must go, I say it's a glory hole, he says it's a storage unit. I could write a book about the contents, which range from a prewar motorbike and everything he has ever found in a hedge bottom, to his paintings, which have become an obsession with him.

It started so simply. The weather had been hot and close with more thunderstorms than I could ever recall. They are always spectacular here, but can be very frightening. Jozef has always been fascinated by storms and cloud formation, like many of the old aircrew are. After one storm, which rumbled and rolled all night, he disappeared on his motorbike. Hours later he returned looking like a one-man removal business, and his new life began. A bag of books was balanced on the petrol tank. A large cardboard box balanced behind him with a dozen rolls of paper and card pointing to heaven like church candles. Boxes and bags crammed with paint and pastilles, brushes thick, thin, coarse and eyelash fine. Pencils, palettes and pots all rattling together. The makeshift lid of the box was an easel, lashed with a few yards of rope around the pillion. The whole image was finished with a large roll of canvas strapped to Jozef's back. I watched as it swayed with every bump and pothole along the miles of paths. I was aghast, he could hardly hold a pencil, how could he manage a brush? I dreaded the consequences.

He retreated into his caravan, immersed himself in books for weeks. Then, on a day with a bright blue sky and clouds that resembled Shirley Temple's curls, Jozef loaded the wheelbarrow with easel, boxes, chair, a bottle of water and a bottle of elderberry cordial. He set of pushing it up the path at the side of the dyke. My eyes followed him, remembering the dark dog days of that terrible time when locked in depression he had walked the same path.

Those early paintings looked like daubs. At first Jozef tried to use an aid that Hans had made for him years ago. Gradually he realised the type of aid he needed and persuaded a joiner from the town to come, watch him paint and then devise one for him. Mr Gresham refused payment and asked if he could buy one of the pictures. He would just stand staring at them. I knew then what was meant by drinking it in. He had been brought up in the dykes and moved to the town when he married. All of Jozef's paintings featured the sky, in all its guises and colours and I had to admit that they were powerful and evocative. Mr Gresham went home with a painting wrapped in a sack under his arm. It wasn't long before there was a steady stream of people coming to buy. Jozef always had a cussed streak and there were times when he excelled. If he decided that he didn't like the person, or they made a comment which he considered inappropriate he just would not sell to them. God help them if they argued with him. There was a torrent of Polish hurled at them and they disappeared fast. It made life interesting.

After the war I managed to buy the cottage and a few acres of land, enough to keep me happy and occupied. A few years later vast amounts of the surrounding land were bought by a huge insurance company. Gradually as the old tenants died or leases came up for renewal, the land was brought under the central control of one manager. He's like God around here. The land is the same but it's used differently. It no longer supports families and communities, it supports shareholders. Its life and soul are dead. All of Jonty's old haunts are gone. There are no farms, as he knew them. The old families have moved into the towns to find work. Those cottages that are still standing are let to people with more money than sense. They come on a summer's weekend, sit drinking and then go. They never see our winter skies, the wind herding then tossing the clouds at a breakneck speed. They never see or feel the driving rain that almost flails the skin from your face, and turns the soil into a thick heartbreaking mud. Saddest of all, they don't hear that special silence, when the air is still, when the sky has a wash of white that merges with frost encrusted branches, glimmers on spiders' webs, and wraps each blade of grass in crystal.

This old house has been my dearly loved home for well over forty years. I know that I couldn't and wouldn't want to live anywhere else. I find myself looking back to the people I have known here and who are, I hope, carrying good memories of us. And I look back to the young man who died in the barn and I wonder more and more, why? I think of Aleksander and the useless carnage of war. Of Phyllis and Jonty who filled this house with love, laughter and compassion. And I think of Frances and the way this house, land, and changing sky caught her in their spell.

Take good care of it when you become its chatelaine, Frances. It's so special, so ageless.

It needs music, laughter and young people again.

It has become such a quiet house.

Salvation

The Journey

I seem to have been travelling all my life and how long that is I don't know. Never could sit to discipline and my Pa was mighty fond of it. I was like a young bronco, biting at the bit. Came the day when the old man took his belt off to me once too often. Enough to say that when he opened his eyes, that's if he ever did, I was gone. Took my horse with me and didn't stop riding for days. The old man would've been so hollering mad he'd have sent the sheriff after me and I would have been hung from a rope for horse stealing.

I thought myself a man and hitched up with a crew driving cattle. I soon found out that I was a boy. The smell of cattle, the dust that rimmed your eyes, that closed your mouth and you were never free of the unchanging dried meat and beans. Worst of all, the goddam loneliness. The hours when the only sound was the movement of cattle and your own cracked voice talking to your horse. You soon learnt to save your spittle for something better than talking.

There was a thread that ran through all the cow pokes and tied them together. Hard, lonesome men, who didn't want anyone at their bridle waiting to be cared for, or interested in their business.

The trail boss was well respected by the cowboys. He was a God fearing man and very fair. He allowed gambling but not for money. Reckoned it was too hard earned and he wanted to end the drive with what he started with in both men and beasts. Oh, we saw folk. Every four or five weeks we'd hit a town, if you could call six shacks, a barrel and plank saloon and two floozies a town. What the men did, he reckoned, was their concern as long as they were ready to start driving at sun up. He didn't touch liquor or women and would order me to hitch along with him. For weeks I had listened to and been teased by the men. All I wanted was to follow their longings and taste both the liquor and the women. Instead, near the saloon there was usually a small tent, but its sign shouted big House of God Welcome Come and Join Us and he made sure I did. Inside the Parson and his wife, smiles splitting their faces, would pump your hand and greet you. There was always food and good coffee and the berry pie was well worth the hymn and prayer at the end of the night. All my life it was a puzzle just how a Parson, a saloon owner, and a couple of floozies knew where there were six shacks in that wilderness, but they always did.

Eventually I got weary of the cattle trail and quit. I wandered north and got myself a new life. I had grown into a loner, content to follow a trail, river, or animal. I took from the land what I needed to live. Any pelts I saved and carried as a stinking mass behind me. If I came across a trading post they would reluctantly exchange them for shot and flour. Often it would be weeks and I wouldn't see a human. I was a true greenhorn but content.

Then came the day I saw my first Injun. I've no doubt the critters had seen me many times. You could feel eyes on you in the forest, I don't know which I feared more, grizzly, mountain lion or Injun. I was trying to get a few more cups of flour from the trader, when the doorway darkened, he lifted his arm in greeting. I whipped my head around and it stayed there. They were not tall men but they were like whipcord, tight and taunt. They raised their arms in greeting to me. I could see interest and amusement in their eyes, then their noses started to wrinkle. It didn't take two shakes of a tail to realise they were asking about the smell, and one shake before a finger was pointed at me and then my pelts. They smiled and then pointed to my clothes and horse. Unlike my Pa, I was slow to anger, but to be jabbered about and laughed at stuck in my craw, it was more than a man should take, especially from heathen Injuns. Slowly I moved a step nearer to them and their hands moved towards their knives.

STOP!

The critters ain't laughing at you … Well, not really.

I stood motionless, staring at them. Each one returned my stare, each balanced on the balls of their feet, each one ready to spring.

No, then what's funny? I snapped.

They're puzzled why you have such a horse, why you can't dress a pelt, and why your clothes are like petals on a flower, quickly gone. They asked if you wished to go to the Great Maker and agreed that if you stay, they will find you frozen into a block of ice in the winter.

I, like a stupid greenhorn, hadn't considered winter. I was further north than I had ever been, had no idea what winter would be like, never mind how to survive it. What a fool I was. He stared at me. I don't know whether it was anger or pity in his eyes.

You've a deal of learning to do … pronto, he said.

He spoke their lingo, they moved their heads, then grinned at me. More jabbering, grinning and heads going up and down. Then it sure turned serious. I stood like a tree stump, staring, watching listening to a tumbleweed of sound. Each had their say, each was listened to. Then all eyes turned and stared at me. I felt like a jack rabbit in front of a rattler.

If a senseless fool like you hopes to make it through the winter, you're going to need help. For some reason these Injuns have taken a liking to you. They have a soft spot for mad people, believing the spirit world is in them. They're going to their village to have a pow-wow with their tribe. If you're in luck and they agree, they'll help you to survive the winter. If not, there's a shack around the back and you can take your chances.

I flushed. All this arranged without so much as a spit from me.

When I said this, Please yourself, was his reply.

They studied me. Five pairs of brown eyes, five pairs of eagle feathers crowning their heads. I wanted to say, I don't need your help, but there was a weevil gnawing at my gut, saying you do, you do.

Three days later they were back, along with two extra ponies. The jabbering started again. I was told that they would take my horse for the two ponies and that the trading post would then sell the horse for them.

No, I spat out. It's worth more than two Injun critter's ponies.

Not out here. It's not the prairie. Those ponies will go where no horse can take you, in ice, snow and bog. They survive months of snow up to their shoulders. His face was red, his voice angry. Keep your horse and die a fool.

We stood glaring at each other. I knew he was right. I nodded my agreement.

Then the clothes you'll need to survive the winter. You'll pay for them with pelts and supply what meat you can. They said they don't expect much, they watched you in the woods. He laughed. A word of advice, try your hardest to learn the lingo and keep away from their women.

Choked, I stroked and said good bye to my horse, my old friend and last thread to my home. Got my rifle and lariat, my bundle and slid my blanket off him. There was understanding in the eyes watching me.

I shook hands with the storekeeper, thanked him for his help and advice and I hesitated.

I'll do my best to get a good man for your horse, he said.

I walked to the ponies, ran my hands along their flanks and looked into their soft brown eyes.

I placed my blanket over the nearest pony. The Injuns watched me as a dog watches a rabbit. I knew what the test was. I managed with one jump and a mighty sigh of relief to get on to the bare backed pony. I nodded to them, they smiled and inclined their heads. The pony took one step forward, I slid off and hit the ground to loud laughter and whoops. They'd known it would happen. It was a taste of what was to come.

Pastures New

I had ridden a horse since my Pa tied me to one when I was three. I was considered a good horseman by other cowboys but I had never had a journey like the one to the Injun village. My education started pronto by trying to keep on a pony without a saddle. They were unshod and moved like a whisper through the grass. There was no sound from the five men apart from snorts of laughter when I hit the ground. I could see no trail or markers, yet just before sundown there was a smell of camp fires and soon I could see a smoke haze and then we were there. I sure was scared.

Children came running from all directions, then pulled up short when they saw me. They stood staring and I stared back. The small ones were skin naked except for a shell or bead dangling from their necks. Ahead I could see the adults, eighty or so stood in a real proud looking group. I sure felt the sweat starting to slide down my face and creep down my chest and back. Hell, did I want to turn and bolt. They looked magnificent and my heart turned to ice. Everybody on the trail says that you can't trust a redskin and here were eighty of them!

For the first months, I was like a deaf and dumb child, a child to be led by the hand. The Injuns were plum sure I was mad and before a day was over, there was a posse of youngsters following me around waiting for the next laugh, and I sure gave them plenty. It started on the first night. I had been shown to a small lodge which was to be mine. Nine poles fixed at the top and walls made out of woven mats and branches of fir. Real snug. So snug, I thought I would strip naked to sleep and tried to recall the last time I'd done this. I was down to my body shirt and even I thought I stunk like a skunk. Then I grew uneasy, I could feel them, eyes watching me, but I couldn't see them. I grabbed my rifle, heard the scuttering as the varmints ran and was in time to see half a dozen youngsters dodging anywhere they could. I bedded down with my rifle that night.

The next morning I was herded by an old woman, her face like an old withered apple, her bird bright eyes guarded, but the start of a smile amongst the wrinkles. She beckoned and I followed like a kicked dog. After a lot of hand waving and face pulling, it hit me that she was to care for me. I was to learn later, that she had been given the task of sussing if I would cause trouble for them. After eating some mush, she laid before me a tunic and breech's made from buckskin. She watched me closely as I stared at them, I knelt and touched the skins, so soft. I stroked the fringing, the fastening lace, and the beaver fur on the shoulders. It wasn't new, but I knew that it had been treasured. I didn't know how to say, thank you, so I stood and bowed to her. She started, then smiled and somehow seemed to grow in front of my eyes. I decided to get rid of my dirt and stink before getting into my new dudes. After more hand waving, I wandered down to the river, sussed the bathing area, stripped and slipped in to the water. Hell it was cold and as clear as crystal. I wasn't a great swimmer, but Lord, I knew I had to move or freeze. That river was teeming with fish and I just swam amongst them. I turned to the bank and stopped. Every woman in the tribe seemed to be washing clothes or children, or jawing to women who were. Every male was checking nets, attempting to spear fish or gutting them. There, plum in the middle of it all, sat my clothes. Like a white man, if they don't want to see, they don't and they had no intention of making it easy for me. The men grinned as I slipped out of the water and scooted for my clothes, the women stared at me, then whispered behind their hands and tittered to each other. The youngsters stood, gazing pop eyed. Now they all knew that it was true, those white men do have hair all over their bodies! From then I was known as White Hairy Bear.

Two of the braves were my special companions. I was sure set on learning their lingo and what was right to do in their village. It was a slow job. They would show me something, say its name then I would tell them the white man's name for it. We did this for a short time every day and before long every child of the tribe was sat there repeating every word. They learnt real quick and it sure helped me. There was always a body telling or asking me a name. They stirred memories of my brothers and sisters who I hadn't thought about for years, I'd almost forgot that I'd had a family. My two buddies also had the job of trying to knock their hunting skill into me. Apart from getting on a horse, there was learning how to use a bow and arrow and then combining the two! Using a knife, skinning, tracking, fishing with a spear, living off the trail in winter and what plants to use for an injury.

I had figured I knew it all and I knew nothing. I would not have survived these winters.

Winter was creeping in and winter would be long. Whether the tribe survived or not depended on what they could hunt, sow or gather throughout the year. From the youngest to the oldest the task was shared, I had half memories of my Ma smoking a ham up the chimney, but these people had to live for a year on what they could harvest. Indian corn was planted and stored. Women and children searched every day for anything that grew, in, under or fell to the ground. Everyday I joined the hunters but the days were getting shorter and colder.

The day came when the whole tribe gathered for the dance, asking the sun not to forget them and to return when its fire was stronger. In my other life, I would have laughed at this heathen belief, but today I shuffled with them, carried along by the beat of drum and rattle, and I prayed to their god and to mine. Two days later the snow came. It was crisp and deep and it came again and again. A furrow was dragged linking lodge to lodge and to the store of wood and animal dung fuel. Woven mats and pelts were hung inside the walls of the tents and life slowed. Instead of living life in the open, it was lived under cover in the warmth. It was a time of watching and I sure learned a lot about them. The love and affection shown to children by the whole tribe, These tough men would cradle a fretful child, play pebble games with girl or boy and wrestle with any boy. I never saw a child smacked. I thought back to the whippings in my own childhood and wondered who were the savages?

There was fun. Singing, chanting, stories of their hero's and gods,. As many bodies as possible were squashed into one lodge. Some tales were so well known that everyone mouthed them with the storyteller! Then that night arrived. It was my turn to tell a story. I had no family or gods to spin a yarn about and they wouldn't have understood me if I had. I stood, mumbling into my beard, with all those eyes staring at me and then inspiration came. I bellowed out Old Macdonald had a farm complete with animals noises. They sure looked stunned, then the children started to fall around laughing, and then the whole pack of them. Gestures were added to the sounds and my fate was sealed. Half an hour later they still wanted more. I tried to think of any others but all I knew were the lonesome songs of the cattle trail.

Slowly the winter passed. We still hunted but by foot on snow shoes. We longed for fresh meat or fish instead of the dry fish and meat strips.

Everything was shared amongst the tribe and as the months passed there was real fear of food running out and the tribe facing starvation. Yet my learning went on. How to hunt fish under thick ice, net a bird, search for grubs, roots, anything that could keep spirit and body together. How to survive a blizzard and read nature's weather signs. At long last the sun crept into the sky, winter was dying. We chanted and danced him to his grave and joyously welcomed the warming sun.

I stayed for two years. My old woman, who had cared for me as a son, became ill. I couldn't move on and leave her; she had become my kin. I would sit talking to her, telling her this and that; she didn't always understand me, but would nod and smile whenever our eyes met. I'd always feared death, no matter what those bible punchers preached. Every cowboy on the trail said they wanted to die with their boots on, but this old woman sure showed me the guts and strength it needed to die in your bed.

At the start of the third summer the tribe was heading north, and it was time I was moving on or I never would. We danced and chanted our goodbyes. They asked their gods to protect me, and I turned my back on the nearest I had to a family.

The Loner

I sure wish I could read and write. I reckon just writing would do, but I guess you can't have one without the other. Us kids had no schooling. Pa didn't believe in it, Ma did, so we had a cat in hell's chance of getting any. Reading's easy, there's always a body in the trading post who would read you a wanted by the sheriff notice or the label on a box of shot. That's the only time a man would need reading. But writing's different. I reckon it's part of you. To see or feel something and put your thoughts down and keep them close to you, they're there for ever. I have seen places so lovely they would stop your heart, animals so caring and gentle with their young that it would make you cry. I would like to have kept a book on my feelings, but I've got no writing. So I did what the Injuns do. I started to make rhymes and then chant or sing them. I liked the chants best, seemed to fit easier in my head and I recalled them easier. They kept me company many a long hour and mile.

Life was mighty good in the years after I left the village. I missed my buddies, but often met one of their hunting groups, or more often they would pick up my trail. We would hunt together for a few days and then part. Always there was some message for me and I would send one back. The further north I rode, the less I saw of them, and I was in another tribe's land. I knew that they would be watching me, but I hunted and camped like an Injun and was sure they would tolerate me. There were times when they stalked and watched me for days, I admit I got a bit scared. Then we would come face to face, always at a time or place I hadn't reckoned on. Surprise in hunting or battle was worth a quiver full of arrows they reckoned. The lingo was often different from my tribe, but we managed. We would share a hunt or a fire. I got into the habit of offering them any carcasses I had. There was a ritual to be followed. I would offer, they refuse, and then when I offered again, they took it, but always a choice piece would be cut and given back to me. There was always a lot of coming and goings between tribes and my reputation had gone before me or rather Old McDonald's had. I got hellish tired of singing it all over the Northwest.

Why I went north the Lord only knows. It's colder, the days shorter and the winter longer, but north I went. It took me some years to reach the Canadian border. I was in no hurry, not meeting kith or kin there. By the time I'd wandered up a few canyons, strayed along a couple of rivers or went to see what was on the other side of the mountain, it would be winter again and movement was slower.

The trading posts were my only link with the other world. Some agents were fair; others were as twisted as a sidewinder and that snake sure is twisted. They stopped trying to cheat the loners after a thieving, cheating, no-good agent got shot by one. They still got away with cheating the Injuns. My pelts were good, soft and clean, and the agents welcomed them, the Injuns pelts were often better. I have bundled mine up and walked out when I have seen them cheating an Injun. The agent would skedaddle after me, saying there'd been a mistake, a mix up. They didn't get chance to cheat a second time. I'd point the Injuns to a post with a more honest agent. Money was like a rifle without shot out there and what's the use of credit marked in a book, when you'll not be going back that way? I would buy shot, flour, salt and, something I hadn't tasted since I was a boy on the cattle trails, coffee! Oh the smell of it. I would get down from my pony just to sniff it in the saddlebag. Last thing at night, first thing in the morning I would sniff it. It sure took me back. The rest of my credit I would take in trade goods, beads, mirrors, combs, knives, simple toys and a couple of colourful blankets. I knew that if I needed a pony or new buckskins I had something to barter with.

White men were mighty rare on the ground. One agent did reckon that every loner was on the run from something, wife, law, debt or himself. If your trails crossed you would jaw over a can of coffee. If they didn't offer a name, you didn't ask it. I think many couldn't recall their birth name it was so long since they'd heard it. Then within a day or so you moved on. Uncounted the years slipped away.

Frenchie became the nearest I had to a pal. Our trails would cross every year or so. He had hunted his way down from Canada and everyone from there was known as Frenchie. He got tired of telling folks that he was Prussian, so Frenchie he stayed.

We drifted into riding and hunting together and for months we would make camp together. Then one morning one of us would be gone. The itch had got too strong. Weeks, months, later we would meet again. There was no need for words, we had travelled so long together that words didn't matter.

Frenchie had been gone for quite a time and I had itchy feet. Summer was coming, I could feel it, smell it, almost taste it. It was time to be off. I had been on the trail a couple of weeks, hunting was good and I felt good. I was slowly walking the ponies out of a stand of trees when I saw it. A small wooden cross and a grave packed down with stones. There were letters burnt into the cross, but all I knew was the letter 6. I stared at it, then knelt and scanned the ground. The earth was still soft after the spring melt, there were footprints, all sizes, men, women and children. What in tarnation did it mean? I edged forward and stopped. The ground was churned and deeply rutted with the tracks of wheels, big heavy wheels and a lot of them. The world was on the move.

I was tying the horses that night, when I heard a rustling in the bushes. I sure lifted my rifle quick. Then I heard his soft, calling whistle. Frenchie!

For once we had a lot of talking to do. He had stumbled on other graves, all nationalities, all ages. He was puzzled and uneasy. Who would bring youngsters out here, where there wasn't even a floozy! He didn't need to track them, he just followed the ruts. A line of great heavy carts such as he had never seen before, slowly creeping along. People of all ages trudging at the side of them. Four or five men on horseback leading, chivvying man and beasts. After a while of watching, he broke cover and ambled down towards them. People grabbed their children and scrambled for the wagons and the horsemen came for him with rifles and guns blazing. I was shocked. What kind of people would do that. Frenchie turned and got out of trouble pronto. A few days later at a trading post he was told a story he couldn't believe. The Government, thousands of miles away, had told people that there was free land and all they had to do was go and claim some.

But that's all Injun hunting land and they believe the land is there for everyone and can't be owned by anyone.

When Frenchie said that he had been shot at, the agent replied, You look like an Injun with your buckskins, bound hair and Injun pony and as far as they're concerned that makes you trouble.

Frenchie shook his head

I don't like it. Why would they shoot at me or an Injun.

We were soon on the trail again. Over the next year or so we heard of trouble between the Injuns and settlers, but we kept heading north. It was early summer and we had just met up again. The years were starting to show, hair grey, a tooth or two loose, sometimes a little stiff getting up in the saddle, but life was good.

We were breaking camp, Frenchie had gone to swill the dixies, when this God almighty scream froze my blood and stunned me for a second. I grabbed my rifle and turned, knowing I would be too late. Frenchie was dead and being torn to pieces by a bear. I raised my rifle, shock and anger at my fingertip. Then I saw them, two young cubs at the side of the she-bear. I lowered my rifle, how could I kill a critter for guarding her young?

Contentment and peace went out of my life. I was restless, there was no joy in the old life. It took me a while to realise I had a hankering to see my old home again. Just like an old Injun wanting to go to his tribal lands to die. I headed south and saw more folk than I had set eyes on in over forty years. I steered my pony's head away from any cabins, I kept well away from any hint of a fort. I sure didn't want to be sport for bored cavalrymen thinking I was an Injun.

It took me two years and a lot of back-tracking to find my old home. I had been little more than a child when I had run away and a child's eyes see and remember differently.

I stared along the dry dusty dirt track, at the hitching rails, the saloon, the church and shacks. I saw the Sheriff's office, the signs swinging and the dry, dusty, dirt road. My eyes slowly passed over it and I realised that I had travelled all those miles and given up paradise for this.

One hell of a rotting, tumbledown, deserted, ghost town called Salvation!

Poverty, poverty

Samuel Hindley

Alright, alright. I can hear thee, I'm coming, stop ringing yon bell, tha'll have it worn out. One of these nights I'll muffle that clapper. Now what does tha want?

We've no room. We're full. We're always full. Most workhouses round here are full. Tha'll have to keep on walking, Mister.

Tha's the choice of two, Melford about 15miles to the right and Bulwick about 10 miles to the left.

Tha'll not get lost, there's well marked lanes going to em. Take a word of advice though. Don't leave the lanes, don't cog over into the fields or woods. If tha does yon farmers will set their dogs on thee, gamekeepers will fire their muskets at thee and both lots are buggers for setting man-traps.

Aye, may be tha's right. I suppose there could be a kind farmer somewhere, but if there is, I haven't clapped eyes on him. Yon begrudge every farthing they've to pay towards the poor rate but there's more farm labourers in this workhouse than any other workmen. They begrudge paying wages even more than rates. Anyway before tha goes I've to enter tha details in my ledger.

Aal tell thee why, because the Guardians of this workhouse say I've got to. It doesn't matter whether tha's entering it or not. If tha rings that bell I've to put thee in the ledger and if tha should be found dead along the road and tha's not in my ledger, I'm in trouble. That's what they tell me but I think it's so they can blame thee if there's any damage, thieving or poaching in the area. So just be truthful when I ask thee anything, mind, I wouldn't know if it be truth or lie, would I?

Aal believe thee. Just let's check what tha's told me. Tha's Silas Foxley, Batchelor. About 38 years old. Parish. Kitterly in Norfolk. By, Silas tha's a long way from home, how long has it taken thee to get here and why? Tha'll not be allowed to stay here or in yon town. Tha'll be run out of the town or have a brick heaved at thee. Tha's no right of settlement here, tha don't belong an tha'll not be allowed to stay.

Tha's looking for work in a coal mine! Is tha mad? I'll give thee another piece of advice, lad. As soon as tha spots one, start running and carry on straight past it and keep on running. Folk come whoame from a mine in shrouds and others leave legs and arms down theer in the coal. Quickest way to make tha bairns orphans is to graft down a mine.

All reet for me! Just what does tha mean? Am the same as thee, a pauper. Does tha think I'd be in here if I wasn't? Folk round here would sooner dee than put a foot over this threshold. I'm here cos the man I fettled for was a drunkard. Owed me wages, stole his customers money, then disappeared, leaving a wife and three bairns. Where are they now? In here, paupers and poorly they are.

No, we don't often get them coming in of a night. We get them trying to get out. Usually those who have lost their mind and them that have never had one. Three one night I 'ad locked up in here. One emptied the ink-pot oower me ledger and ruined it. Guardians didn't take to that. They said ad have to pay for it, so I towlt em to knock it off me wages. Seeing ah get nowt, they didn't like that neither.

Folk are at their wits end before they'll come here. If they've young un's they'll come in sooner when it's cowld. In the mild weather they'd sooner sleep in the hedgerows an in winter they creep about the streets and alleys, they starve and dee theer.

I've a bit of bread and a couple of cowld tatters, tha can have a bite as long as tha mouth isn't ter big.

No, nowt else. If tha's clemmed tha'll eat owt. There's some count them-selves blessed if they have a plate of nettle porridge in a day. Make thee mind up. Does tha want a bite of bread and a tatter afore thee's on thee way? If not, it's Good Neet to thee.

Billy Boots

Billy Boots, Miss Grant-Bullen.

I was baptised William Cotter, Miss. I look after all the boots and shoes in this place. Everyone knows me as Billy Boots, Miss.

What do I do Miss? I take their footwear when they first come in, mark them with their number, tie em together, put em on the shelves, men's on one side, women opposite, children between.

Yes, Miss, all of a person's possessions, except a woman can keep her wedding band. Why? I couldn't say, Miss. We're not allowed opinions, Miss.

Perhaps it's as you say, Miss. They want us all the same, like a flock of sheep.

I'm sorry, Miss. I must have misunderstood you.

The army, Miss. Thirty years, most of that time in India or Burma, Miss. Ten years in here, Miss. Oh yes, you have to work for your bread, Miss, the Parish makes sure of that.

So I understand, Miss. Times are hard, people have cause to be frightened with all these soldiers wandering the highways There are men trying to get in here every day saying they're old soldiers. I soon sort them out.

Nothing as complicated as that, Miss. A soldier's boots are special to him, a matter of pride you might say. He'll keep em clean and polished even if it's only with his spit. Begging your pardon, Miss. Another army habit, he'll always put dubbin and blacking on the bit between the heel and sole of his boots. So it's easy to spot a soldier when you know.

Yes, Miss, some do find it very hard in here. They don't like losing their boots for one thing. Take Sergeant Henshaw, fifty years in the army and a chest full of medals. He'd sold some before he got here.

For food or more likely drink, Miss. He was dying when he came in but his boots gleamed. When I had to take em off him I felt bad. He made me promise to take care of them and I did.

What did I do, Miss? I blacked em and buffed em every day, cleaned the soles and the leather laces. Then I'd take em to the infirmary ward for him to see.

He'd just smile and rub his fingers on them. Then after a few weeks he died.

What happens to belongings? Oh it's simple. If you walk out of the workhouse door you get all your things back. If you get carried out, the Parish sells everything. Not that they get much, Miss.

No. I couldn't let that happen. Not to the Sergeant's boots. So I gave em one last good polish, you might say in his honour. I went to Charlie Martin in the mortuary, he sees to the bodies like I see to the boots. Charlie was an old soldier, he knew what was to be done. The Sergeant went to which ever battleground he was going to with his boots on. I couldn't let anyone step into those dead men's boots. Could I, Miss?

Grace Brownsword 1

Come on, stop nattering. Tha know's Mistress always comes down this corridor when we're scrubbing it. Why we've to bottom it twice a week when there's only her, Master and the Doctor allowed to use it I don't know. Six flagstones wide, the whole length of this God forsaken place and me and thee bent double on our hands and knees for hours. Then she struts along like Jezebel.

I'm saying nowt, tha'll find out soon enough and if tha's any nous tha'll keep it to thi'self.

How long in here? Too long, I can tell thee. Three years and thowt I'd go barmy many a day. Tha'll get used to it lass…. one day. It's best to keep tha' eens and lugs closed in here. Tha'll spend all thee days and neets fretting if tha don't.

Tha's reet, it's perishing. I've more chilblains now than when I was a child in the fields. There's neither coal, food, nor clothes to keep out the cowld in this God forsaken place. Then they hand us a pail of icy watter to scrub this passage with..

Oh, we all fettled in the fields. Dad worked for Farmer Clough, who thowt well of him. No hiring firm for me Dad. Five childer and we grafted from being reet small, scaring birds. picking stones, fetching cows in, letting them out. At harvest time, we gleaned, flailed, carried, planted, picked, and sorted. Mrs Clough saw the chilblains on me hands and legs. She just said, 'Grace, with me.' She never called me Gracie, always Grace and I liked that. Into the house we went and that's where I stayed.

Me Mam and Dad say owt? Nay, what Farmer Clough or Missus said were law and it meant they'd one less mouth to fill.

I'd be nearing seven. Me eens were on stalks for weeks. I'd never seen owt like it. Missus said we'll make the beds and I stood, gawpey as an idiot waiting for hammer, nails and wood to help make a bed.

Thou can laugh lass, I can miself when I think back. Mam and Dad had a bed, them at the top, and two little un's at the bottom. Missus had a big bag filled tight wi' feathers on her bed an' a body sank right into it, and white sheets covering it. Missus said I'd to call em 'bed linen'. At whome we had old sacks wi' straw in. A slept in a kitchen cupboard at the farm. Tha opened doowers an theer was a little bed. Eee it were strange at start. A were reet frit by misel'. Missus let one of farm dogs come in wi' me 'til a were scratty wi' fleas.

Eh Carrie, tha's nosey for a young lass. Aye I got wed, to one a farm lads, Harry Brownsword. I were but fifteen, he eighteen. He were a gradely man, gentle and kind. Missus liked him. Tha'll not do better than Harry, she said and she were reet. The farm had workers cottages … do tha know Carrie, they never once put a widow or anyone too old or sick to work out of a cottage. Nan Bridger had been a widow woman about three years when we wed. Missus arranged for us to move in with her. It worked well, we kept a watch for Nan and she for us. Harry was the sun, moon, and stars to owld Nan. Me and Missus had many a laugh bout it.

Nay lass, a carried on working. A were reet good at butter and cream making, Missus said a could knock her into next week at it and she were a good un. Farmer Clough got a few more milkers and we were at it every day and market on a Saturday. The dairy earnings kept the farm going through many a bad harvest. It were at market I first come across Mistress, only she'd nowt to do wi' workhouse then. She owned 'The Turks Head.' Tha can pick thee chin up off floower Carrie. Tha don't know everything, lass.

Am saying nowt, Carrie. Yon walls have big lugs and a lot of folk have big mouths.

Oh aye, we had a bairn, about two year after we were wed, we had our lad Dick. We were reet happy with him. A'd have a lump in me throat as I watched Harry cradle yon babe in his big rough hands. Nor but weeks old an he'd be telling bairn abowt hosses an cows an birds he'd noticed.

Aye, an I hope tha does find a man like him.

It would be abowt two year on and I was expecting again. I was still working in the dairy and owld Nan looked after Dick. If she loved Harry, she worshipped Dick. Life was good but like every other farm labourer, tha knows it can't last and it didn't. It started when Saul Clough got wed.

Why didn't a talk abowt him afore? Cos he is lower than vermin. He married Leah Dutton the only child of a farming family but she'd no intention of being a farmer's wife. No dairy work, preserving, baking bread, caring for orphan lambs. She was going to be a lady, even bought a silver bell an squatted in front parlour rattling it for afternoon tea! Missus soon throttled that. Everybody has to graft on a farm if it's to make brass. Farmer Clough spoke to them both and there was angry words, then no words. It was terrible. Then the owld man fell to the floower, he couldn't talk or move and deed next day. Poor Missus, it was if she'd turned to a cob of ice.

Sithee here, Carrie we've done nowt but natter. She'll be here soon so let's get stuck in.

Am saying nowt else abowt her, Carrie, no matter what tha asks. So get scrubbing, lass.

Tha's reet, it wasn't long afore there were changes. My Harry reckoned Saul had gone around with his eens and brain closed for thirty years. There was one blessing, we had a baby girl and called her Nancy after Nan. Dick had been bonnie but Nancy was beautiful. We thought life was looking up, instead it blew up. Shsss. A can hear feet. Put thee bucket up against wall and stay tight agin it or yon woman'll kick it ower. She will. Keep scrubbing and ignore her.

Hey! tha's trod on me fingers and afore tha says it were an accident, I know it weren't.

A couldn't miss it, Carrie, I've seen that smirk on her big ugly face many times. She's evil, an the sooner she gets to hell the better. She likes being cruel and my eens are on her, and she knows it …

I don't know why tha's so keen on my life, it's the same as other folks. There's a lot of hurt and pain and talking about it doesn't make it less raw, lass. It doesn't make it any easier to live it again. Harry weren't well, hot, sweat slaking off him, coughing and couldn't breathe. Young master walked in ter house and said Harry was to be working next day. I tried to tell him Harry had been clearing mouldy hay and if he gave him a couple of days he'd be better. Two days later he put us out the doower and …

That's just it, Carrie, they can. Work for them an they own thee. Missus was heartbroken, she'd pleaded with him and does tha know what he said to her. We want thee out of our farmhouse, and in that cottage by the end of the week. I thowt she were going to dee. But she stood straight, looked at him and poured curses down on him. He were shocked, we all were, I could hardly breathe or believe what I was hearing. It was as if she cursed somebody every day of the week. All I could think was, that curse came from the bottom of her heart and her a God fearing Methodist.

Well, believe it or not, it's true. We watched Harry trying to breathe.

71

Missus had two tears easing down her cheeks but she was the first to move. She went to the stable, harnessed Milly and backed her between the shafts. She walked past Saul with her head high and came out of the farmhouse with a couple of blankets and a basket. We'd got Harry and our few belongings on the cart when she joined us. They spoke not a word to us. The farm door shut, Missus flicked the old pony and we lurched down the track.

Grace Brownsword 2

The babe was sleeping in the potato basket wedged across the corner of the trap. I could hear Nan and the Missus talking, very quiet, their anger gone, just bewilderment left. Harry was laid on the floor, his head resting easy on my legs. His eyebrows were spiked with sweat, his forehead, nose and cheeks ran with moisture.

What did I do ? What could I do apart from wipe his poor face and try and get the thick bubbling fluid out of his mouth. His terrible coughing tore me in two. I could see nothing but his face and his eyes fixed on my mine. I knew he was dying and so did he. His sweat had a smell of autumn, a touch of ripeness and rot. At one time I'd loved the smell of autumn. Eh, I'm sorry for crying, lass.

Aye, as you say and I know, life does goes on. I knew that no family, no matter how Christian, would risk sheltering a dying man coughing and hacking the way my Harry was. Our only hope was a spot in an inn's stable, even a publican can have a thread of charity in his heart. Day was edging into night when we saw the flickering candles in the windows of 'The Turk's Head' and I started to pray.

Oh, tha does interrupt, Lass. I were too frit to plan anything. Missus said she'd wait to see if we got shelter. I'd never stepped into an inn afore. I'd allus been told they were Satan's playground and the men that used them his disciples. Nobody had ever mentioned what the women were called. The smell and smoke set me coughing and my eyes streaming. Through my tears I could see folk laughing, childer staring and a woman at a table with a big book and a hard look on her face.

Will tha stop thee screeching and jigging. Aye, it were her. As fat as she is now. Bright red frock that hardly covered her nipples ncer mind the rest, but it were her face, I couldn't stop staring at it.

It were painted, lips bright red, eyelids painted green. Rest of her face were like putty, except her cheeks. Yon looked like two red cabbages. I've only seen painted faces on hiring day, tumblers, clowns and the magic men. I couldn't take my eyes off her. Hair thick and black as a tar bucket. Her eyes stripped me as I walked towards her. I stared back and somehow asked for work. She pulled a face like I were vermin, then screeched loud and hard. Everything went quiet, nobody breathed and we all looked at her. She smirked, then turned her thumbs downwards. Afore ….

Aye, I did wonder if it were a wig, seeing that it's the colour of a bag of carrots now. There's more to come, Carrie, if tha'll only let me get on. Afore I could open me mouth this man stood in front of me and gave her some coinage. She marked something in her book and gave him the nod. He went to a bench were these childer sat and beckoned one. She stood and I were shocked stiff. She were nor but a mite, no more than six or seven and she'd nowt on but a little shift. She stood like a lost soul as he eyed her up and down, he nodded and led the bairn through a doower. Tha can call me thick but it were only then that I knew what the benches of childer and women were for. I took one step towards that painted face and didn't get chance for a second. I were dragged between the benches and they all started stamping their feet and jeering till I were thrown out.

What I did? What does tha think. I stood, shaking. I sobbed me heart out. The babe was whimpering, and I put her to my breast, my tears falling on her face, my gulps of breath catching hers, unsettling her. I could feel Harry's eyes on me, duller, more vacant than before. Nan took charge of us. 'It's the Workhouse, lass,' and I knew what she had always known, it was our only hope.

What did I think when I saw it? All I saw were this great black wall as high as an oak tree, an I'll tell thee something else, it were hard to find a way in, but Nan did. The gate man were reet good to us. He looked at Harry and decided we should stay with him for the rest of the neet. More peaceful, he said. He carried Harry like a babbie and laid him on a sack of chaff. I sat on the floower agin him the baby across my knees. I knew he hadn't long, Carrie. I wanted to be with him, I didn't want him to go alone. We were all there, me, Nan, the gate man, who only knew Harry's name. The workhouse buried him next morning in a pauper's grave. It broke my heart.

A know, luv, there's nowt anyone can do. When tha comes in here, the world disappears.

I found miself working in the kitchens. Eight ounce of bread a day, gruel, boiled beef and boiled spuds twice a week, soup five times a week, it's hammered into my brain. When Nancy was weaned she had to go into the children's block. Oh Carrie, what a shock. It's four floors up, the children are never brought down into the fresh air. The little ones that can walk are tied into wooden chairs around the walls of the rooms and are tethered there all day. It's the old and the mad who look after them. Them as need looking after themselves. I saw one owld man hit a child and another eat a child's dinner. Do you know, Carrie, you can only see your child for two hours a week. I went to see the old Mistress and pleaded to see my two children more. She refused, said it was the rule and marked me down as a troublemaker.

God alone knows who makes the rules up, lass, but they don't have to live by them. I know life got harder. Charlie Martin came to see me one neet. He's the mortuary man, Carrie. He asked if I knew Nancy was being buried the next morning. I didn't even know she was dead. Charlie has a key to every doower in the place, as he said, you never know when or where people choose to dee. Like thieves we crept to the old people's block and collected Nan. Clinging to each other we followed Charlie. In the candlelight the mortuary was full of shadows, I peered through them looking for a coffin and saw a small rough box. Charlie said something to me as I moved to it but I didn't hear his words. He lifted the lid and I looked in and didn't recognise my child. Her face swollen and bruised, eyes black and clumps of her hair missing. She were fifteen months old.

Nan and me didn't go to our work the next morning but stood by another pauper grave. We watched four wooden boxes and last of all a tiny one, my daughter, lowered in. I swore I'd find who had abused and killed her.

It wasn't long before I was found out. 'The new Mistress wants thee' came at me from all directions. I was beyond caring. I knocked on the big heavy door and walked in at the tinkle of the bell. I recognised the fat woman at once and she recognised me. She stared at me, then that smirk slid across her face. Slowly her thumbs pointed upwards, then just as slowly turned and pointed down. War was declared.

Jonty Parkes

Nah then, Stumpy, it looks as if he's put us together. I don't reckon much to that. If tha thinks it's me doing all stone picking tha's another think coming.

Tha what? Who telt thee that?

Mr Bickerstaffe? Now I know that tha's a liar. Yon's the hardest man round here. He'd skelp anyone who wasn't doing their work and I'm warning thee he uses a big 'ard leather belt and he doesn't care where it lands. Scaring birds, tha'll never lift yon great big rattle. How old are thee anyway.

Seven! tha's only the size of a bantam. Birds'll laugh their yeds off at thee. Swing yon rattle an tha'll knock thee knob off. Here let me have a go.

Ooh me lugs, they're ringing, Stumpy. Tha needs to shove some moss in tha lug holes or tha'll be deaf as a door knocker.

Me, I don't rightly know, nine I think. Me Mam were a gin swiller, allus too drunk to talk. She deed and they put me in workhouse. I'm being sent out at Michaelmas so I must be near ten. I'm going to work at Mr Barretts stables.

I know nowt about hosses, I'm frit of em. They're too big. Billy Boots sez I'll have to perch on a bucket to hook a nose bag on critter. I want to be a soldier, take Queen's shilling like him... Hey up, Boss's coming. Get rattling an I'll leg it through yon hedge and get picking.

He's away. Tha nearly raised the dead wi yon rattle, Stumpy. He'll be back though. Why does tha talk funny? Is Stumpy tha reet name? Was thee born with half an arm or was thee in a reet good fight like a soldier?

What does tha mean it's us what talks funny? Thee hardly opens thee gob when tha talks, tha tongue and teeth won't fall out tha knows. Eee lad, don't start skriking, Tha'll wash all muck of thee face. Tell thee what, give rattle another go, then tell me thee name and what happened.

That's bad. Orphanage shouldn't have split thee from tha sister and sent thee here to mill. That's not reet, it's no wonder tha's only little when tha's been stuck neath a loom every day. So what happened?

That's not reet neither, Alfred. He shouldn't have kicked thee into yon machinery just cos thee weren't fast enough. Aye that must have hurt. Did tha scream thee yed off? Was there blood all over the place? Eee I bet it hit the ceiling and run all down the wall. I hope it hit yon man, smack, reet in the een. What's tha skriking 'bout now. Tha's a reet babby. Theer's pigeons at top of the field, time for thee rattle lad. I'm back to picking stones a'fore owld Bickerstaffe creeps up on us.

Am reet sorry Stum, I mean Alfred, for making thee cry. I've never met anybody with their arm cut off afore, can I touch it? No, just end on it. Aye, don't start off agin. Tha'll need to be tougher if tha wants to join Army wi' me. Oh I'm fair clemmed Stum, sorry, Alfred.

Thee doesn't know what clemmed is? Hungry, lad. Starving. Me belly telt me it's time for our snap.

Dry bread and some watter from yon ditch. Hey up, tha's got trouble. Tha's got to get down to ditch, an tha's only got one hand to hang on to yon bush and cup tha watter. Tha'll have to sup from mine or use thee clog for a mug. Come on, belt it down, owld Bickerstaffe's on the prowl. Did tha sken birds go up down there? It's him. Owld devil's pushing through yon hedge.

Well fancy, him giving thee some bits a spice, if tha hadn't give ge me one I'd not believe it. Eh, Alfred it tasted gradely, reet made me chops watter. He were nosey, ferreting all that out of thee. Nowt to do wi him.

He's after something or going soft in yed. Tell thee what, tha can come with me again, Alfred. Bread and dripping, spice, cake, am not fussed what he hands thee.

Alfred, as tha knows, some of lads think they're cock of the midden. All they want is ter thump and scrap. Cross me heart I'll braid em if they touch yer. There's only daft Ned I can't lick and if I tell him Mistress'll thump him he'll not touch thee.

Tha don't want to know her. She looks at yer and tha wet tha kecks. Little Polly reckons milk goes off when she walks in kitchen. She's nasty, keep out of her way, lad. I've just thowt on, I maun be getting puddle, Alfred. If we shape reet, we can sneak into men's room and see Charlie Martin and Billy Boots. They showed me how to feit like soldiers do, clean and dirty, Billy said. Tha'll teach thee to feit and look after thisel and telt thee if there's any men with one arm in the army. I know there's one legged uns cos Charlie telt me he made a wooden leg for one of his mates. Hey, we could ask him to make thee a wooden arm. Then tha'll be able ter feit an come in army with me.

Bessie Liddle

Lizzie, I thought she was going to kill me. Thud, crack, she was hitting me with the besom, on my back, arms, anywhere she could land it. The whole time she was shouting and screaming and spit was spraying out of her mouth like a …

I didn't, honest, Lizzie. I didn't do anything. I'd been sorting the washing out and heard a crash and the Mistress shouting. I knew it must have something to do with Maude. I ran in and oh Lizzie she was stretched out on the flagstones and the Mistress was laying into her with the brass milk pan.

It's true, honest, I must have shouted cos she turned and looked at me. She was like a mad woman. Her face was red and seemed to be twice as big, and her eyes, oh my God, I've never seen anything like them. They were like frog's eyes, all round and bulging. She wasn't saying anything just grunting like a pig with every blow. Then she ran at me.

I know she's big and fat, Lizzie but she can move and she did. She flung the pan at me and it cart wheeled all over the floor, then she grabbed the big besom…

I'm trying to tell you what happened if you'd give me half a chance.

Maude? She wasn't moving, just laid flat out on the floor with all blood on her head and face. Mistress stood on her when she started after me and Maude still didn't move. Oh Lizzie, I think she's dead.

It's easy for you to say stop crying, you weren't there. You haven't had to put up with the shouts and blows from her since she came here as Mistress. You can't do right for doing wrong with her.

What did I do? I ran up that passage like a scalded cat and all I could hear were her feet pounding after me. The next thing the besom flayed across my neck and my head hit the wall. I staggered and the next thing it was slicing down on my shoulder. Oh it does hurt and I can't feel my arm, Lizzie.

Why didn't I …? Are you mad, how could I take it off her? She's three times bigger than me and in case you've forgotten she's married to the Master of this workhouse. All I wanted was to get to the back door and out of it. I wasn't quick enough though.

I know it's hard to believe, her being the size of a prize bull but it's true. I reached for the door handle and she landed another one, this time on my head. I was trapped between the corner of the door and wall. The next thing my head's grabbed and she's pounding it on the doorjamb. I could feel her breath on my neck and her grunt every time my head hit the door jamb. There were people shouting and banging outside, I thought I was going to be safe but they couldn't open the door with me wedged against it.

I don't rightly know what I did, Lizzie. I know I was screaming and kicking on the door and I lashed backwards with the heel of my boot. I must have landed her a good one on her shin. She gave a hell of a scream, grabbed my hair then started clogging me. I just rammed my elbow into her belly, I think I winded her.

You shouldn't laugh and say that, even if it's true. She was doubled up in pain but still hanging on to my hair. People were still shouting and trying to open the door. The next thing, Billy Boots was there. I don't know where he came from or how he got there, I'm just glad he did. What he did to her I don't know but suddenly I could move me head. He took hold of me and wanted to know what had gone on. I could hardly tell him, me teeth were chattering and I was crying so much. He made me sit down as he said before I fell down. I wanted to be sick. Oh Lizzie, he's going to be in such trouble. He was swearing at her, then he grabbed hold of her right rough and dragged her to that little privy outside the Master's house. He gave her such a shove and in she landed on her big backside. He jiggled the latch out and she's locked in there. Then he sent someone to fetch the Doctor and the Master and told old Sara to bring me to you.

No, I don't know where the Master was. He was in the kitchen when I left it. Maude was trying to keep the table between them. I shouldn't have left them, she's always saying don't leave me if he's there. He must have heard all the screams. Why didn't he come and stop the Mistress?

Aye, they reckon she's the boss. If she were as they say the landlady of the 'The Turks Head' she'd be more than a match for the Master. All I know, he was in the kitchen when I went out but not when I got back. I think he's scared of her like the rest of us. Oh poor Maude, she tried to keep her distance from them both, the Master with his wandering hands and the Mistress with her twisted tongue.

Oh Lizzie, what will I do if Maude's dead. What's to become of me? I've nobody else.

Martha Taylorson

Come pretty one, come pretty one,
come, come, come, come.
Come to my garden and
whistle and

Eee Charlie Martin, I should have known it was thee and tha wagon. I could have saved me breath. Tha wagon sounds different, heavier, it rumbles more. Mind you this corridor is as big as a church and twice as cold, not that I know owt about churches me being chapel.

What am I doing here? Dodging work and having a nose around. I were knitting socks from eight in the morning till gone five at night with fifty other old women. This week it's teasing oakum. My fingers are raw, my arms and shoulders ache and me yed aches with the smell. So I'm stretching my leg's and I'm reet glad to see thee.

Me get in trouble? Don't tha fret about me. I enjoy putting my nose where it's not supposed to be. The secret is be hard faced, Charlie. It's simple. If a think anybody's about, tha'd think I'd escaped from yon mental ward. Me mouth opens and out comes the singing, not too loud but loud enough to be heard.

Oh, one of yon mucky song's tha picks up here and thither in life, the kind a lady shouldn't know but a soldier does. Anyway who's tha carting off in th'owld meat wagon today.

That's sad. Who delivered the poor lass? God help the bairn in here.

What do I do after me song? That depends who's stood there. If me serenade doesn't make em trot t'other way, I embarrass em, nobody likes that, it soon shifts em. That new young doctor just smiles at me. As for the Mistress, I march up to her, and rant at her because she hasn't curtsied to me, her Queen. I put my hand out for her to kiss.

What does she do? Tha should see her face, it would stand clogging. She made to hit me across me face one time. So a told her, I'd have her head off or see her hanged if she dared. She'll have me one day Charlie, I know that.

The Master? He always hurries away sooner than pass me, especially after last week.

Aye, al telt thee and be reet glad too. You and Billie Boots keep your mouths buttoned and I trust thee. Am reet worrit abowt one of the young lasses. Tha might know what's to be done. A were at top end of this corridor and as tha knows it's dark up theer not like bottom end. A saw Master wi this scrap of a lass, I thowt, thee's up to no good. He unlocked doower of yon room, an she followed him in like a new born lamb, then click and it were locked again. I knew what were in his mind. A went as fast as me gammy legs would carry me. Before a got theer, a could hear lass crying for him to leave her alone. I banged on doower and was yelling to the child. All a could hear between her sobs was stop it Master. He didn't say a word or open the doower, so I started screaming.

Why screaming? That's easy. It were the only thing a could think of and am reet good at it. The young lass joined in, she really rattled the windows. The door opened and she was shoved out. It were slammed shut and we heard the key turn. Lass was reet upset, buttons were ripped of her bodice, she clung to me shaking and sobbing in a reet state. I've got to tell somebody and put a stop to it, but who, Charlie?

No, Master's said nothing to me. Not him, he sent somebody to tell me I'm on disorderly diet for a fortneet for breaking the rules. The food's bad enough without being put on disorderly. Tha knows, Charlie, food were bad afore these two come but it's a sight worse now, an I can tell thee why. The Master is the brother-in-law of Seymour Jarrett, the Guardian who happens to own Peacock's Wholesale. Not many folk know that, anymore than they know Mistress is Jarrett's 'bit on the side' and has been for years. It were always well hidden. Tha's been a soldier, Charlie, tha knows what she is. She owned the Turk's Head for long enough and still does on quiet. Am not saying it wasn't a knocking shop afore she came, but never little childer or boys. Jarrett is the money behind it.

How do I know? Aye, Charlie I didn't always look like this. A were a bonny looking lass and by the age of twelve a were out in the big cruel world. A wanted to go into service, tha knows learn to be a ladies maid. Trouble was, they thought I was too much of a temptation for husbands and sons! So I earned my living as one of the girls at the 'Turks Head'. There were ten of us, we lived there like a family. Some wed, others moved on, most of us kept in touch. When a couple of us got too old for the game we rented a little shack near the canal. As we'd got older so had our regulars, they'd turned into friends, too old and stiff jointed for frisking. Not all of em though. So they'd come, bring a jug of stout, a bit of bread and cheese, some cold meat. Harry the coal man always brought a bucket of coal. We'd have a game of cards, talk about the old days. Some of the happiest times of my life. The lasses that were still working at the Turk would come with all the gossip and scandal. Then Jarrett bought the Turk for Her. Within a couple of months the girls we knew had left and it was all change.

No, she weren't wed then. A shock to em all when she walked in with the Master. They might as well stayed single from what the lasses said.

How do I know? The owld girls brought a couple of the new ones along, then they brought others and the gossip starts. The tales they told about her. She was beating the childer and set about the girls if they tried to stop her. They were sure she sold some of the childer to bawdy houses.

How did she get to be a Mistress of a workhouse? Simple. Master and Mistress of a Union House have to be wed. Jarrett's a Guardian and has a big say in who gets the job, and he is a Wholesale Grocer and Ironmonger. He had his mistress married to his brother-in law in no time. Within a couple of weeks of them being in charge of the house Jarretts goods are coming through the doower. Grace Brownsword worked in the cookhouse and complained to the Mistress about oatmeal that was dross, rotten spuds, flour full of weevils. Two days later she's owt of the kitchen and scrubbing floors ten hours a day. Her little lad's been sold to a mine owner wi' nine others and not one over seven years old. I'd like to know how her lass came to dee as well.

I think tha's right, Charlie, there must be more too it. I've thowt about it a lot an I'll tell you what I know. As well as Mistress skimming money off provisions, clothing and the rest, she's doing something worse. Think of the Liddle girls. She told them she'd train them for service in a big busy house. 'The Turks Head' is big and busy. I reckon as far as she's concerned a workhouse is champion for a good supply of young fresh girls for a bawdy house. No one asks after them, they don't cost the parish a penny. The fact she killed one won't put her off but I'll find someway or other to stop her.

Oh Charlie, I could kiss thee. That's taken a reet weight of me mind. Just find out if Billy and Sam Hindley know owt abowt Master an Mistress and what they're up to. Are thee sure about Dr Sinclair, I can't understand a word he says and he mightn't believe us. He's that young, he's hardly grown two whiskers on his chin yet, but if thy says he's all right and he'll know

what to do and how to stop them, that's good enough for me. I must get
…. Shush- shush- sh there's somebody coming, It's her –

hum.
Come to my garden and
we'll have some … fun
Come pretty one, come pretty one
Come, come, come, come.

Merita Pinder

I'll tell thee this Ella, these November nights are doing nowt for my chest and knees. Am creaking all over like chapel doower. Tha can see yon skim of watter on walls, it'll be ice be morning. You mark my words.

What do does tha mean, tha gets used to it? I haven't and I've been in here three years. What's time tha done in here, three weeks? Thy mark my words, in a couple of weeks tha'll creak in every joint and watch thee breath freeze afore thee face. I wish they'd give us a hot brick an a bit of old blanket to take to bed. We don't even get a warm drink. I miss my warm watter going to bed.

Nay, I'm not a widow woman. Me husband's up in th'owld men's ward still breathing and moaning. He were fair chuffed at us being separated in here. Said he'd had enough of me carrying on at him and looking at me miserable face. No moaning, no nagging, no wife he said. An I thowt, yea and no slave at thee beck and call all day and all night, me owld cocker. He thowt there was a snug in here for th'owld men just like at the Red Lion. It were set in his yed there was a gill of porter and a twist of baccy every night. He were in for a shock The owlder yon man got the more nowt and awkward he got. I never thowt I'd welcome coming in here but I did. I've peace now.

What did he do? Give him his due he were always a grafter. When we first wed he were a farm worker till they sacked him.

Tha might well ask. He were a dreamer. All that interested him were canal that ran through the farm. His plough never need sharpening, hosses stood taking weight of their feet all day, while he stood watching barges going through. Oh farmer were reet with him, give him a warning which is more than many of em do. Next morning he were whoam, sacked. He were sat watching barges before milking had even started, didn't even sken Boss watching him. I'd have sacked him meself.

Just take a sken at that scorrick of a fire. Nowt but slack, no heat in it. They should have it sat in middle of this big room, we could all hunch round it than.

Tha' don't feel the cold? Tha' soon will when tha covering of fat drops off.

Any how, my man got a job, night soil man. Tha' has to be reet clemmed to do yon and we were. Farm cottage gone, growing plot gone, four childer, an we were on path to workhouse. We lived in and off the hedgerows, then winter set in and we knew we had to get into yon town. We begged, knocked on doowers, sang outside pubs and Joe pinched any food he could get his hands on. We knew it were a gibbet job but what could we do? We were beggars and tha's no choice. He were four years a night soil man and there wan't a minute that we didn't all stink of it.

Why does tha want to nose into our family, what's thee up too? I'll tell thee this bit, then tha mon tell me your life, reet? Every morning when Joe finished work he'd walk up to the canal lock. Happens he thowt he could leave the stink thee're. He got to know yon lock keeper and would give him a hand for an hour or two. He didn't seem to heed the stink of Joe, neither did the bargees. Joe reckoned that between em, they dumped so much soil and rubbish in watter, it stank more than him. He took himself yon one morning but keeper were missing. Joe found him in the lock. He were reet fond of a drink, Joe said. Seems he were piddling drunk neet a'fore, fell in lock and drowned. Joe and one of the bargees shinned down lock gates an fished him out. He were a big fella. Joe reckoned if he weren't dead a'fore they started hauling him out, cracking his yed half a dozen times on gates soon finished him! Then Joe got stuck in and cleared the queue of boats in the basin. The canal bosses offered him the job and we were there till three year ago when he broke his leg. The horse quack set it crooked and it didn't mend reet. Owld devil were seventy and bosses said enough, and on your way. They give him half a sovereign and he drank the lot. It were the workhouse then. The canal saw our childer all reet. The two lads are lock keepers and lasses married lock keepers.

Am I happy in here? What does tha mean by happy? I know there are some folk better fed in here than they were outside. We had a growing plot that he took good care of. Joe wasn't easy to live with. He liked rules as long as they were his, tha knows what a mean. 'Thou shall not ...Thou shall ...' I always bristled to em and it got me many a back-hander. I'm the same in here. Why should I wear a cotton bonnet even in bed when I'd never even owned one in all my life? Why must I wear a dead woman's shoes that cripple me when I've always gone barefoot or in clogs. Why must I go to church or chapel on a Sunday? It's all what I must or must not do and there's no sense in most of it. But I do love the company. To sit knitting with twenty other women, knitting pins trying to catch up with tongues and sometimes a song or two, that's nearly worth the cowld. I've never lived near so many people and I like it, even at neet, wi' snores, coughs, and shouts. I lie in me little box next to thee waiting for sleep and planning what I can do about that new Vicar.

Nay Lass, tha must have heard. Since last Master and Mistress got their reckoning, it's been the only buzz round here. I don't know where they dug yon Vicar up, but they want to gerr'im back there quick, 'im an that Miss Grant Bullen have come up wi daft idea that owld married couples should not be separated. As Vicar said to me a nice little room for you both to share. I towld him what he could do with it. He's chelping at Doctor Sinclair, I heard him 'the bible says, What God has joined together let no man pull asunder. Yet the workhouse does.'

I'll tell thee this, Ellen, if they do start it and they condemn me to being at that old man's beck and call, rubbing his knees, rubbing his back with camphor oil, listening to his farts, belches, moans, and snores, dodging his nips and wandering hands, I'll kill the old bugger or burn the workhouse down!

Come on, old lass. There's the bell, eight o'clock, time for bed and I know nowt about thee yet.

Charlie Martin

I used to enjoy a drink in the White Hart, Billy. It were a good ale house, quiet, clean, no trouble and they brewed a gradley stout. I can still taste it even if it is four year since it last slipped down my gullet. Every night I was there, yet I never saw the inside of that upstairs room.

No, I don't think anyone was banned from it, but it was always kept for meetings and of course the magistrates court.

You might well ask what meetings. I never saw a soul go up nor come down, sometimes you'd hear feet shuffling or voices but never what they were saying. I wondered if it were these workmen who want to unite into confederations. Matt Butler the landlord will be in trouble with the magistrates if I'm right. He was always on about the fraternity of the working man.

You're right, old friend, there's not been much fraternity in the workhouse the last two years, not that there was much before. If it doesn't improve after listening to that evidence today, it never will. But then, no one takes any notice of us.

What did I think of the court today? I'd have sooner been downstairs in the snug with a pot and a pipe. No seriously, I've never been in a court, well not a civilian one, many an army one though. When they said the Magistrate was Sir Edmund Billingham I wasn't happy. He's reckoned to be a hard bugger. He owns half the county, so every poacher before him knows its transportation for them.

You're right, he didn't waste time, straight in and to the point. He was speechless a couple of times and I don't think that's happened often in his life. When he asked the Master where his wife was, and he said 'We're not married.' The gasp was enough to blow the roof off. Then when he said 'It was a pretence to make sure we got the job of supervisors of the workhouse'. Did you see Sir Edmund's face, I thought he was going to have a fit. He was quick though, 'Who arranged that?'

'Guardian Seymour Jarrett and my so called wife, his mistress'.

Then the next scandal was that Jarrett had paid Guardian Jaynes to keep his mouth shut.

What a buzz, the town people knew they were in for a good show after that. Better than the hiring fair and dancing bear put together. There's Jaynes demanding we go to church twice on Sunday, hanging all those religious tracts on the walls and he's there getting his palm greased. We were thinking we knew everything that went on in here, but they kept that well hidden, Billy.

I won't argue with you on that. Truth will out, and it certainly did today. When Dr Sinclair told us what he was going to suggest to the magistrate, I thought no one, especially Sir Edmund, would agree to it. But he's a hunting man, it's the start of the season and once the Doctor explained it would speed proceedings up, Sir Edmund was hooked.

Don't you think it made it like a play, Billy? Dr Sinclair explaining the Poor Law Commission rules and how they were ignored or broken in the town's workhouse. Then everyone involved in that specific incident said their piece. Sir Edmund certainly wasn't letting anything past him, the questions came fast and thick. When he was satisfied he moved on to the next. It was like turning a page over or the next scene in a play, a horror play. The Doctor's way made it easier to tell our story. Take Grace Brownsword, I looked at the lass and thought, all she had suffered in the workhouse. She was so pretty and healthy when she first came into the house, nought but a young lass…

May be eighteen, nineteen years as you say, Billy. Look at her now, twenty one, twenty two years and looks nearer fifty. The Doctor had certainly thought out the next scene. When he said, being new to the job he thought he'd check the death register. Did you notice how quiet they all went? His shock at finding that over half of children five years and under, died within six months of coming into the workhouse. I'll tell you something, the crowd didn't like that. The money folk were shocked, the poor were angry and ready to hang someone. He went and saw the Mistress, who showed him the food plan which seemed adequate but he soon found it wasn't as it seemed and the scene was set for Grace.

Aye, you're right, she held them in her hand. Not a sound, as if they didn't want to draw breath and miss a word. The provisions from Jarratt's Emporium at top price but dross quality. Flour that was half chalk and crawling with weevils. The infants milk watered down till it looked like water that a blue bag had been dipped in. Stinking meat that was green and full of grubs. She missed nothing out and told it well. Then her punishment for daring to complain. Nobody in that room will forget her telling of seeing her baby daughter's body covered in bruises ready for burial and she not knowing the babe was injured never mind dead. When Sir Edmund asked who could have injured the child and Grace described the situation, the folk in that room were so angry. You could feel it, almost as if they wanted to march and put a keg of gunpowder under the workhouse and that lot of villains.

You're right, Sir Edmund was as angry as everyone else. He really tore into the Master, who just blamed the Mistress for everything. When Sir Edmund asked the Doctor how this could happen the Doctor was straight and truthful. He said he knew nothing about the child, its death or burial, until told by Mr Martin a week later. Master and Mistress seemed to consider it not important to inform him but the Mistress had filled in the Death Book giving the cause of death as convulsions. No, he didn't think it would have been convulsions. Yes, it was against the rules for them to enter anyone in the death book.

He said in the short time he had been employed there he had complained about the care of the young children on numerous occasions. The two capable women who had cared for the children had been moved to the washhouses, being replaced by an old woman and an imbecile man. He had since been told the man could be violent.'

When you think Billy how many times me and thee have been bit, thumped and kicked as we struggled with others to put the straight jacket on Johnny. Him near babes, I wouldn't let him near a mad bull.

I don't know who's idea it was or why, they didn't know Johnny for sure. It was no wonder that when Grace started to tell about her daughter and young son the tears came.

How could he be anything but gentle with her Billy? She was so upset. I didn't think he had it in him, Billy. Arrogance yes, understanding no. It brought it home to everyone when she said, 'We're country folk and can't understand how anyone can sell a child, never mind a six year old child for three pounds. Send them to work in the dark of a coal mine for fourteen hours a day. Country folk don't sell their children.' What did you say, Billy?

I suppose you're right when I think about it. As you say, some must have done, farm workers have always been half a step from starvation and the workhouse. I'm told these pit and mill owners can tell a good story and folk think they're giving their bairn a chance. It seems the poor are always the losers.

You reckon about thirty children have gone, sold, since they arrived. How do you work that out, Billy?

Well that's simple but not all children come in here with shoes on their feet, in fact most have never had shoes in their life.…

Why didn't I think of that. Your shelves have a store of shoes, so thirty children have walked out of here wearing dead children's shoes. All you have to do is count what you had and what you've got left.

As for the money they were paid for the children, none of it came to the House. Master was right about Her dealing with bills and money. She was always in that office scribbling away. When he was asked where the money was and answered, 'The Mistress dealt with all the money and knowing her it will be in her pocket' I thought old Edmund was going to pummel him!

He was shaking as he roared 'That's the problem with you, you bastard. We don't know where her or her pocket is but I think you do.'

I think you're right, old soldier. That shout from the public area shocked him. He's started to realise he's facing the long drop and hopes to twist out of it by telling all he knows. This magistrate is no fool. What do you think, Billy, the assizes?

Well, you may be right on both counts. He was shocked to see her. I'm sure they know each other. She had that amused half smile on her face, as old as she is, she's full of mischief. Martha told me herself that she was one of the 'Ladies' at the 'Turks Head'. You mark my words, Billy, there's something between them. She sat like a purring cat, not the old wayward woman she is. She told her tale well and her suspicions about the Mistress's plans for the young girls. That caused a rumble. I think everyone agreed with her. When Sir Edmund started to question the Master I think he'd sooner have throttled him. Do you know, Billy, I can't believe we didn't spot all this was going on. When Master said how many young girls he'd 'trained' I could've been sick. When folk started shouting he'd have been wiser keeping his mouth shut, instead of yelling 'It's not against the law.' Did you see that old fella lift his blackthorn to him. Doctor should have let it land. I don't think any of this would have happened if the women and children were allowed to live together. Women would have protected the children, boys and girls.

I've never had a child, at least not that I know of. I would have been proud of one like young Bessie Liddle. Nine years of age, tiny but she coped. I watched her face as she told how Master hounded Maude and bullied her. One of the women should have sat with her when she described the Master's tricks to get to Maude, and the Mistress's violence. It's not right, that poor child having to stand up in front of two hundred people, living it all again. Seeing her sister being battered to death, having to run for her life when the Mistress turned on her. Is it any wonder we could hardly hear her for the sobbing. Poor, poor, lass.

As I said to Sir Edmund, someone got that privy door open and let the Mistress out and she was away. There are only two people who would do that. The Master or Seymour Jarrett who hadn't signed Samuel Hindley's ledger so definitely wasn't in the house.

Sir Edmund didn't waste time. Some magistrates would have brushed it under the carpet ….

Or had their hand greased. He just glared at him and bellowed, Assizes, Quarter Sessions.

The Master's realised he's likely to hang for someone else. He let everything out, every theft, abuse, rape, intimidation and now murder. Every soul in that room was stunned. We were, Billy, and we knew more than most. I just hope they find that woman soon.

Aye Billy, I'm tired and weary but with that feeling that something right has come out of the day.

Amos Critchley. Guardian

Before we start the meeting, I would like to welcome and introduce the Reverend ffinch-Allingham in place of our loved and much respected Reverend Grant Bullen, who has resigned due to ill health. Reverend ffinch-Allingham is the nephew of Sir Edmund Billingham. I'm sure he will be a great asset to the workhouse and will be happy with us.

The first item on the agenda is the appointment of a new Master and Mistress to the workhouse. I'm sorry to report that there has only been one couple applying for the post. The Board of Guardians feel most strongly that there must be a greater choice of candidates. We cannot risk a repeat of the last four years. The newspapers both regional and London have been asking for progress on appointments. We are going to ask the couple recommended by the Parish Church if they will continue until we can appoint permanent replacements.

We pay £80 per couple plus food and lodgings per annum. To increase that, Reverend ffinch-Allingham, is to take away from the inmates and there is little enough for their needs.

I can assure you that life isn't a bed of roses in here, Mr Armstrong. I'm sure that you are aware that most of our inmates are the old, the very young, the infirm and lunatic paupers.

Yes, the poor harvest and weather conditions have led to a small increase in admittances but not as many as expected. I hear workers are being sacked and evicted but none have sought admission yet. It isn't surprising considering the trouble that has been associated with the workhouse. They will be desperate and in a sorry state when they do come.

I can't agree with you, Mr Armstrong. We have a Christian duty to care for those in need. I know that you and the other mill owners felt you were unfairly criticised for the alleged exploitation of pauper children. I'm sure we all at times resent the amount of Poor Rate we are forced to pay. Contrary to what many people think, these paupers do not choose to be ill, old, crippled, orphans or insane. There is no joy in living in a Union Workhouse I think you would agree. We have a lot of business to go through, so if we can continue.

I would think about another hour, Mr Leadbetter. I have requested refreshments, which can be served now if that will help. Peppermint often cures, I'm told. Some of the old female inmates do have some strange remedies, which I for one would be very hesitant in taking.

I can't help but agree with you. Descended from witches, especially those from the farms and moors.

There is a rumour galloping around the house that our elderly couples are to be housed in their own rooms with an allowance of coal, tea and sugar. No matter how desirable this may be, we have not got twenty-three small rooms nor the finances to provide coal etc. for them. There is not one iota of truth in this.

Doctor Sinclair has been called away to the infirmary. He asked me to read his report. Before I do, I would like say that Doctor Sinclair, from his first day here, has requested a separate sick room for children and women, also a separate room for infectious illnesses. All our sick inmates are nursed together and by other inmates who are often highly unsuitable. Dr Sinclair has requested permission to train a small group of suitable inmates in the care of the sick. I feel that we should individually give this request careful consideration before we meet to discuss it. Now to the report. I feel that we have important lessons to learn from it.

3rd July. I called into the large infants' room only to discover that five of the infants had severe diarrhoea and vomiting. I had not been informed of the situation. It was obvious that it would spread rapidly and endanger the remaining fifty infants.

The temporary Master felt he did not have the powers to take the actions I requested. He informed the Guardians, who to their great credit immediately granted them. I had requested a room as near as possible to the large infants' room. The inmates in the secure room were quickly and safely moved to a smaller room in the lunatic area, which has since been made more secure. The original secure room was well scrubbed and cleaned. I requested Mrs Grace Brownsword, an inmate, and nine other women of her choice to be released from their work to care for the infants. I gave them detailed instruction and the reasons for them, then transferred the five infants and two of the women there. The large room was scrubbed from top to bottom. The two rooms and the women and infants were then completely isolated from the rest of the house. The disease did spread rapidly and it is thanks to our ten women that not more infants died.

Doctor Sinclair reports that twenty-one infants died and thirty four survived. These are better results than expected.

I totally agree with you, Mr Leadbetter. Dr Sinclair is to be congratulated. I understand that without the isolation it would have spread through the rest of the house and all age groups very quickly.

On behalf of the Guardians I will congratulate Doctor Sinclair. I also feel that we should examine his ideas closely.

Other Business, Gentlemen.

1, Ordered that the overseers of Crank be instructed to take out a Warrant for the immediate apprehension of the husband of Mary Blunt for leaving his wife and four children chargeable to the parish of Crank.

2, Sarah Winter a pauper of Haresfinch Parish has been delivered in the Workhouse of a bastard child of which John Wraith, a farm servant, is the father.

Ordered that an application is made to the magistrates in Petty Session at Billinge to make an Order of Affiliation.

A cheque of £2 and six pence be given to Mr Lister the Master of the Crank workhouse for the funerals of three indoor paupers.

Richard Thompson	Eighteen shillings.	Adult.
Jacob Fletcher	Eighteen shillings.	Adult.
Ann Wraith	Four shillings and sixpence.	Child.

We have obtained and served a Magistrate's Order of Maintenance against John Fowler of Luton for three shillings weekly towards the support of his father, James Fowler, a pauper chargeable to the Parish of Eccleston.

Are there any other matters you wish to be discussed, Gentlemen?

I would be obliged if we could have informal discussions with Dr. Sinclair during the next month. I would appreciate knowing any dates that are not convenient for you.

You will of course, Mr Armstrong, be able to raise those points with Dr Sinclair. Hopefully it will be a discussion not a confrontation, Mr Armstrong.

That concludes the meeting for this month, Gentlemen. Supper is ready. Thank you.

Doctor James Sinclair

I ndeed, Reverend Grant-Bullen, a sorry state of affairs but at least justice has been done. Death for the Mistress, transportation for the Master, prison for Seymour Jarrett and Tom Jaynes. The court appearance was an ordeal for everyone from the house. They longed to be back here. Can you imagine anyone longing to be back in a workhouse?

Oh no, you mustn't feel guilty about the happenings at the workhouse. You were ill and had nothing to do with the appointment of those evil corrupt people. Coupled with Seymour Jarrett they had carefully planned their crimes. It's hard to believe that people can behave that way.

I'm quite sure you're right. The people were incensed when they heard how the infants were treated. And then preparation of young girls for prostitution... Seven people reported where the Mistress was hiding. That's unheard of in this town and shows the depth of their anger. I suppose the mine and mill owners are rattling on your door. They are angry that the London newspapers are full of the trial and their involvement in the sale and poor treatment of workhouse children.

Did you know that Sir Edmund attended all four days of the trial? It created quite a stir when he marched in. I suppose that comes with money and his position in society. It was obvious that the judge knew he was coming. They smiled at each other like old friends.

No, I didn't know that you were all first cousins and had been brought up together, but then I'd no reason to know ... nor that you had been at Oxford together. A good trio, one to care for the soul, one to care for the body and one to protect their wealth! A good family practice, if you don't mind me saying so.

Sir Edmund made an unannounced visit to the workhouse yesterday. As you know he has no jurisdiction over us. In fact the gatekeeper refused him entry at first!

Are you all right, Reverend? I thought you were choking. His steward nearly had a fit when told in no uncertain terms that nobody could be admitted without being entered in the ledger. When the steward retorted it was Sir Edmund stood waiting, the reply was 'He can be the Duke of

Wellington or old Nick but his name and yours goes in my ledger before you enter.'

Are you sure you wouldn't like some water, Reverend?

Oh, he was in great humour. As he said 'You can't fault a man for doing his duty'. He then demanded to be shown every inch of the workhouse. I had no objections. It was good to see it through his eyes. I've grown accustomed to the gloom, cold and stench of it, which is remiss of me. The distaste on his face when he saw the mid-day meal bordered on the humorous.

Barley soup and dry bread. I gathered he is fond of his food. He remarked that the midday meal for the whole workhouse wouldn't pay for a family breakfast at the Hall.

Was there anything he thought satisfactory? Nothing! He was scathing about the infants' room. Appalled at dormitories with sixty beds that held the old, the infirmed, the mentally defective and the able bodied together. The fit men, women and children were either working at tasks in the house or rented out to farms and local employers. The old and infirm men and women were trying to unpick oakum. He was shocked when he saw what was involved. In fact I believe the whole visit was a shock. Both he and his steward recognised some of the old people as former workers.

No, that was the strangest part. He nodded to one or two of the inmates but didn't speak a word to anyone, then in the women's workroom asked if he could speak to Miss Taylorson. That really caused a buzz with our old women, they reminded me of a flock of fledglings, heads nodding and mouths chirping. It reinforced the impression I got at the trial that they knew one another …

Reverend, I'm dumbfounded. Is this another tradition of the English upper classes? That young males of related families are raised together, almost as a cohort, I can almost understand. That at the age of fifteen - each one is marched off in the care of the head stable lad to be initiated at the local brothel. Why?

Good heavens! All three of you with Ruth Taylorson … known as Lily. Someone was a romantic to call all the prostitutes after flowers.

I'm speechless. My Father is a minister in a Kirk and I know what he would say about it …

No doubt your uncle was right, it did help to protect the parlour maids and keep bastard babies from the door!

Oh, they spoke in my office for about fifteen minutes. I think the women would have fought to get their ears against the keyhole if the steward hadn't placed himself in front of it. When Ruth returned she was obviously irritated. She holds her tongue well and all she said was 'If he thinks he can tell me what to do, he can go to hell.' The chirping mouths dropped open, eyes darted everywhere and the shock and excitement was palpable. A bellow summoned the steward and thirty minutes later I was called.

Absolutely right. You certainly know your cousin, Reverend. He asked how I would like to see the workhouse run and within a few minutes we were at logger-heads. As I told him more than once, he has no jurisdiction over the workhouse or administration of the Poor Law.

I would say his colour was more purple than beetroot, especially when I said that the inmates should have some means of representation on the Board of Guardians. 'You cannot have the rats in charge of the ship,' he said. He would not accept that it might have prevented some of the happenings of the last two years. I suggested there should be at least one woman on the Board, he retorted that a workhouse was no place for a lady. I pointed out that many ladies actually live in it. Mr Kirton, his steward, has a persuasive tongue and Sir Edmund listened to him. I explained our infants are penned on the third floor. We let Sir Edmund have the idea of moving them to the ground floor. Within seconds he was agreeing to a gallon of milk daily from the Home Farm and fencing for a grassed area for the infants. Mr Kirton knows how to handle his Master.

We agreed on a great deal and argued on a great deal more. Your cousin is a stubborn man. He is against a school, maintaining it gives people ideas above their station. He will need some persuading on that. I thought he was going to have an apoplectic fit when I suggested opening the Infirmary to the poor of the town. Again Mr Kirton's suggestions came quietly and reasoned. I do wonder if he was a workhouse child, he is so aware of the life and needs of our paupers. I have agreed to chart my ideas and would like to involve you, Reverend.

Yes, a lot of work, but a chance to develop better care for our paupers of all ages.

Of course, I will have a dram with you. The toast ?

An end to Poverty?

New Worlds

March. 1849

My Dearest Sister,

I miss you so much. It is strange to feel so lonely when surrounded by so many people, but they are not my kin. In my mind I tell you about the strange happenings and the people we have met. But most of all I tell you about my fears.

We arrived in Independence, Missouri a month ago after a long, dirty journey. It is a strange place. Wooden buildings, most not much bigger than sheds. The few sidewalks are made from roughly hewn wood. The air is hot, with a sandy dust always swirling and spiralling around us. It makes it difficult to breathe and our skin and clothes are coated with it. Over all this is the stench of livestock, thousands of them.

John is full of excitement and hope. The prairie schooner as he calls the wagon will soon be ready. We have our provisions. I have never seen so much food, or vittles as people here call them. 300lbs of flour, 100lbs of bacon, 30lbs of beans, even half a pound of baking soda! The list is endless. I wonder if there will be enough room for us! We are joining Mr Nesbitt's wagon train and leave next week. How I wish we were going back to New York and home. John signed a list of rules that we must obey, such as no drinking or gambling, no more than ten head of cattle to each family and no single women! I told John that as a newly married woman I wasn't worried about that. The rule on cattle has led to some families leaving our group. One family had 300 head of cattle and four cowboys. Mr Nesbitt warned them that they would be lucky if 50 of them survived to Oregon. They didn't take kindly to that and are joining a train which has many more wagons and a few thousand beasts.

John is out most of the days. He is talking to everyone he can find about the care of livestock and wagons. We must be the most inexperienced of people setting out on this journey. The days are long and lonely for a woman without kin living here. I decided to visit the one and only store in the town. It is small, wooden and bleached grey by the sun. It was hard to walk or find the counter in there, it was so stuffed with goods. There were tins of kerosene, sacks of salt, sides of bacon, sewing needles and everything else to go into a wagon, but no luxury goods, not even a jar of candy and I have such a longing for some. I could feel eyes following me around the store and it made the hair on my neck stand up.

Are you the new doctor's wife? a large woman behind the counter barked at me.

I shook my head and thought her one of the rudest women I had met No, I'm travelling to Oregon.

Her eyebrows shot up, I don't know if it was due to amusement, derision or incredulity! Her eyes slowly travelled over me. From the tip of the pink feather in my hat, over my second best dress and rested on my crocheted gloves.

Not dressed like that, I hope. You'll never get there.

I could feel the anger rising in me but she just carried on speaking.

First of all get rid of that corset you're wearing.

I stared at her speechless with shock. There wasn't a day since I was thirteen years old that I hadn't worn a corset.

Then get some loose drawers and cotton clothing, you'll find skirts and shirts the best. Oh, and a shawl and a couple of sun bonnets …

I gasped, and clutched my little pouch bag. Did she think I was a farm girl? Before I could speak she carried on and a stout pair of boots. Oh, and an apron.

I was incensed, turned on my heel and walked out of the store, I hope with my head held high!

I expected John to support me when I told him how I had been insulted. He just shook his head and gave his little half smile.

Listen to what people here say. They know and understand what the conditions will be like. The old life has gone, it's the start of a new one.

There was little choice at the store, two bolts of fabric, one calico, the other cotton. They appear not to take any measurements and one size is sewn for all women. I will soon be the reluctant owner of two calico skirts and aprons, three shirts and sets of drawers, a shawl and two sunbonnets that I would be ashamed to own in New York.

Please don't tell Mama, she would have a swooning attack if she knew that her youngest daughter would be dressing like a washerwoman.

The last two days have been terrible. Mr Nesbitt came to inspect what

John calls our wagon.

I doubt it will ever be that to me. He wanted to know what kind of horse trap I had driven. When I answered that Papa had never allowed me to drive, he swore, then asked if I knew how to fire a rifle or a shot gun. I shook my head. He swore again, turned to John and said Teach her and make it quick.

I don't know if this letter will ever reach you. I'm entrusting it to a pastor who will take it as far east as he is going, then it will be passed along a chain of unknown travellers and hopefully reach you.

We start to assemble on Friday and Mr Nesbitt will make a last inspection of our soon-to-be home. There will be twenty-five wagons in our train and it is planned that we will start our journey to Courthouse Rock at 4am on Monday.

Meg I am so frightened.

With deep affection
Your loving sister

Isabelle.

May 1849

My Sweet Sister,

I have lost all track of time and have no idea of the date. I am not even sure of the month.

I was so excited when I saw in the distance the massive Jailhouse Rock. It took us so long to reach it I thought it must be a mirage hovering in the distance.

Oh how disappointed I was to find no letter from you. John argued that there hadn't been time for my letter to reach you, never mind a reply to travel the thousands of miles between us. He pointed out that no one in the train had received letters. I pointed out that very few could read and those who could were either Dutch or German. Please write as soon and as often as you can.

Tell me all the news even about the cat and the mice in the kitchen. How are Mama and Papa, is Mama still having the vapours? Will you tell Cook that I dream of her roast beef and her blueberry pies. Are there many recitals and concerts this season? I am so homesick for the sidewalks, the theatres, the stores of New York, but most of all for my family. I ache to hear the laughter and voices of home.

I'm pretty good at harnessing the oxen and my driving is improving slowly. I suffer a lot of teasing when I talk about harnessing oxen. Even the children tell me that oxen are yoked and horses harnessed. The children think it great fun to watch me struggle with yoke and straps.

We saw our first herd of buffalo last week. We were warned that they spooked easily and stampeded at the least noise. Mr Nesbitt thought there were over a thousand beasts. We hardly breathed as we crept past them, partly through fear and partly through the stink of them. The children sensed the danger and gathered close to their parents. The livestock appeared to tip toe through the grass as if sensing unknown danger. Even the creak of the wagons and the jangle of the straps seemed more subdued. Then over one hour later we were past the last of them.

I am getting to know the other travellers, or pioneers as we are called. In the first weeks I thought them rough and uneducated, which some definitely are. Yet it is I who am uneducated in the art of survival. I thought that I would be able to pay one of the women to wash and cook for us. I was soon told in no uncertain manner that one of the reasons they were on the trail was to get away from people like me. I tried to watch how Martha, a big noisy woman cooked. She came at me like a whirlwind. She accused me of spying on her, which I suppose I was. I started crying, she held me and couldn't believe that I had never cooked, washed clothes and only done fine sewing. She has taken me under her wing. I now know how to make flat bread on a hot stone, how to cook beans and do something that I hate, washing clothes. She has become a real friend.

We came to our first river crossing five days ago. Meg, I had been dreading it. When we got there it was worse than anything I could have imagined. A large wagon train had arrived before us and I now know why John decided not to join them. It had already taken six days to get eighty wagons across and that left another twenty wagons and over one thousand head of cattle to cross. The river banks were very steep and the men had hitched logs and strong chains to the back of the wagons to ease them down. There were men pulling, whipping and kicking the beasts trying to get them down the banks and into the water. At the back of the wagons there were crowds of men hanging on to the chains hoping to stop the wagons from careering down the bank, overturning and killing or injuring both men and beasts. The men were up to their thighs in the sucking mud and it was dripping off every inch of their bodies. The most harrowing part was the panic and screams of the children as they clung to their mothers or any struts they could reach in the wagons.

Some of our children started crying, I suppose panic is catching. It brought home to us as we watched just what we had undertaken. Mr Nesbitt called the men together to say that he had decided we should travel along the river bank for another day and then cross. I'm sure if the women had been consulted they would have said turn back. It took us one long day to get wagons and beasts across the Kansas River without mishap. The men were so tired that we were late hitching up and starting to roll the next morning. They were mighty pleased with themselves though.

The day after this we met our first Indians. They seemed to appear from nowhere. Within seconds, all the men and a lot of our women were holding rifles or guns. I just stood there with my mouth open. They were smaller than most of our men with long hair and just wearing breeches. They were most unpleasant, pointing and demanding food. Mr Nesbitt came and barked at them in what seemed to be their language. They didn't seem to like what he said but after another few shouts they went. Everyone was on edge for the rest of the day and the guard was strengthened that night. I must confess I sat on the bedroll with a shotgun on my knee when it was John's watch.

I think it will be very difficult to go back to the corsets and fitted clothing we are expected to wear in New York. I felt embarrassed and uncomfortable when I first wore these country clothes. Then I felt ashamed at thinking I was superior to my friends who have helped me so much. Then after a week or so I realised that I liked wearing my loose-legged drawstring drawers, my loose cotton shirt and skirt. That I could walk and move freely, even bend over. I was cooler during the day, yet my shawl was ideal for the sudden coldness that comes so quickly at night. However I just can't bring myself to wear the apron, Meg.

We are travelling towards the next staging post, which is called Chimney Rock. Mr Nesbitt said we will never forget it but won't say anymore. At fifteen miles a day it will take a while to get there.

John says I should forget time, that it means nothing out here and we should just live for the minute but I find that hard to accept.

Please write and tell me all the news and particularly if there is any gossip. I want every scrap of news on the family. I love and miss you all so much.

Your loving sister
Isabelle.

May-June 1849

My Dear Dear Sister,

Today, a small group of Indians came riding towards us. As always the men reached for their guns and the women reached for their children. We waited hardly daring to breathe. I don't know why we react this way towards them. There has only once been any problem with a very small group when they were begging. The others we have been in contact with either ignore us or come to barter. Usually they want sugar or clothes in exchange for dried berries, fresh meat or their clothing. Our men have realised that the Indian trousers are virtually indestructible.

We watched closely as a package was handed to Mr Nesbitt. Oh the anticipation when we realised it held letters, I can't describe my joy when there was one from you and the dejection amongst my friends to find they had none. Some cried and I cried with them. There was only one solution and that was to read my letter to them straight away and I have since repeated it five times!

I had to describe your cream ball gown in detail. Attempting to describe silk to women who have only ever seen or worn calico and thick cotton proved impossible.

They were intrigued to know why there was a ball for the Foundlings Home and why Mama is angling to get a place on its committee. They laughed when I described the power and influence of Mrs Sylvester and they all agreed that it was no different from them trying to keep on the good side of the Doctor or Parson's wife.

I am so pleased that you are back to your old self and Mr Osbourne is still visiting. I think you have a beau, Meg. What does Papa say and more importantly what does Mama say about him? She must like him otherwise Papa wouldn't have been allowed to give permission for him to visit!

You are right to chastise me. I haven't mentioned John very much. He is well, in fact I think you wouldn't recognise him as the same man who worked in his father's bank. He is burnt brown by the sun, and seems to have developed muscles everywhere. He is loving this life and always asking the other pioneers why, where, and how. I'm sure he will be able to do any job when we finally arrive in Oregon. He just brims with life and enthusiasm and can't understand why I get homesick.

It is hot, dusty and slow walking. I am sure that we fall asleep on our feet in the afternoon. I know the sway of the wagon lulls the driver to sleep. Ruben Appleyard dozed and fell from his wagon and broke his arm. He hollered to the sky and hollered even more as Mr Nesbitt set it. Three men including John had to hold him down. John got bit on his backside, Jonty Parr was bit on his arm and Thomas Shmitt got a kick in the face for his trouble! Their language was colorful.

His wife Aggie now has to drive the wagon and care for six children. It is strange the way people here don't have to be asked to give help. They just see the need and give it. I can't see our friends in New York doing a neighbour's washing. It has been brought home to me yet again why it is so important that the women can drive these huge heavy wagons and be able to shoot.

We have arrived at what must be the strangest, most unbelievable place on earth. In the last few days the horizon we have watched for months started to alter. Instead of being straight and flat as usual, it started to have dips and bumps. We were sure it must be distant hills. Each day they got a more definite shape and gradually they appeared to be houses of a soft, red colour. Then we decided as they continued to get larger that they must be palaces, yet we knew they could not be. We were still some miles away when we realised that they were huge sandstone rocks rising out of the flat prairie. I don't think anyone of us could imagine such wonders. They have names like Jailhouse Rock, Courthouse Rock, and then the wonder of Chimney Rock. It resembles an upturned funnel with the spout rising hundreds of feet into the sky. Mr Nesbitt spoke the truth, it is awesome.

I've told you how John has changed. He has to see, touch and examine everything for himself. I knew what he was thinking as we finished our meal and the quiet of the evening was creeping in. I was right, it wasn't long before he'd persuaded the other men to ride and view those sandstone wonders. When they had gone and the younger children settled for the night, we sat around the fire. There was a song or two and idle conversation that some how drifted into ghost stories. We were conscious of the eerie strangeness of the rocks, they seemed to have a presence that was there with

109

us. The stories became more and more frightening. We all had our shawls pulled tightly around us, through fear not cold as Mary started to tell of the Banshee her mother had heard and seen. Our eyes were on her as she held us transfixed. Then we became aware of a wailing, low and threatening, gradually it grew louder and higher then there was a screech that froze our blood. It was answered then drowned by the screams of twenty-five women and a brood of older children. Scream fed on scream. The younger children, eyes glued with sleep added their piercing, frightened screams. Then came the sound of ghostly hoof beats. It's those savages from hell come for us, Mary cried. The screams took on a new life. We started to run, then stood terrified as horses shied and plunged around us. We heard familiar voices and our men launched themselves from the saddles. They wrapped their arms around us as we sobbed on their shoulders. They'd heard our screams as they were returning to camp and thought Indians had attacked us. They risked life and limbs to rescue us.

It didn't take long for Ruben Appleyard who was cowering in his wagon too admit his sin. The men were so mad he was lucky not to have his other arm broken. The women were hopping mad not least because we felt so stupid. He received a lashing from the tongues of twenty-five angry but relieved women later - it was a topic of great merriment amongst the men and some freely admitted that in Ruben's place they would have done the same. Of course they didn't say this in front of their wives.

We leave Chimney Rock in the morning heading for Fort Laramie and then Independence Rock, which is the start of us leaving the prairie. I am told it is the half way marker.

Take care of yourself dear sister, I long to see you.
All my love
Isabelle.

Something terrible happened yesterday. One day from Chimney Rock. Jannie the youngest of Martha's children was killed. She was thrown out of the wagon when the wheels sank into a huge rut.

Her mother's screams are still ringing around my head.. The child was dead when we reached her. Martha cradled the child and said she wouldn't leave her here alone on the prairie. They both know the train must move on and they can't survive alone but it must be hard to part. Her Pa scraped a shallow grave out of the baked earth and laid her in it. Martha pleaded for the child's resting place to be marked. A piece of flooring was prised out of their wagon and Mr Nesbitt scratched onto it

Pause stranger and offer a prayer for Jannie Gebbie who was three.

Her Pa hammered it into the ground and we said our goodbyes to her. We moved on the next morning with a silent Martha and husband. This is a hard cruel road.

In great sorrow,
Isabelle.

July 1849

My dearest sister Meg,

I have read your letters over and over again, I know them by heart, but just touching your writing brings you closer to me. I could imagine all the family happenings as you described them but I must be becoming a Pioneer as I didn't envy you all the concerts and balls. Well, not too much.

I was the only woman on the train to get mail. They all yearn to be in touch with their old family life, and without news of theirs, mine will do. I read a few sentences of your letters to them, then the questions flowed. It soon became obvious that it would be easier to read every word of your letters to them. They know my family nearly as well as I do. Listening to their family stories has made me realise how privileged our life has been. Very hesitantly I was asked if I would write letters for them. I looked into their pleading eyes and couldn't refuse. Like Mr Nesbitt I have set some rules. I made it clear that twenty letters can't be written at a twenty- four hour trading post stop. I suggested we make it ongoing. If they thought of something to say today, we would add it to what was written last week. They liked that idea. Then finally, they would provide the writing paper. Since then Meg, I have written on brown paper bags, scraps torn from packaging, even a label from a sack of seed potatoes! No doubt I shall be reading the replies. It's not easy to understand a lot of what they say, in fact I can understand Greta from Holland better than a most of the American women. They start every word with a yawl and forget to pronounce the rest.

You asked me to describe our day so that you can imagine what it is like. Most days are like the one before.

I'll start with the prairie. It's often a magical place. Vast tracts of grasses that you can see no end to. There are no trees to break the horizon. The colours of the grasses shimmer and blend together in the sun and the flow-ers are every colour in the rainbow. It moves and seems to change colour to every breath of air that we can't even feel. As it ripples it murmurs and sings, at times plaintive, other times a lullaby. Over it all, is a sun that beats relentlessly from when it rises until it sinks. Martha describes it as peeling the skin of your eyeballs. There is no shelter from it.

We rise and eat at four o'clock and have broken camp and are walking by seven o'clock, even the children. The very young ones do have occasional rests on the tailgate, but the wagon is kept as light as possible for the sake of the animals. At every opportunity the wagons are pulled into a river to try and stop the wheels drying out and breaking. The oxen are usually determined that they are not coming out of the cool water and the men's tempers get frayed and language ripe as they try to drag them out.

The heat of the afternoon is ferocious and travel is slow. About five o'clock we make camp. By this time we are coughing and choking and coated with dust. If we are lucky there is water near and modesty is forgotten in the need to be clean and cool. Then a hot meal of salt bacon or meat and anything we may have found along the trail. The little ones are often so tired that they can do nothing but fall asleep on the bare earth. At times we are too tired, lonely or homesick to do anything but watch the sun go down. Other times we sit around telling each other our dreams and hopes. Some times singing will start and soon it's those quiet songs that bring hope and yet longing to us all. There is one song that was totally unknown to John and me, yet everyone else seemed to know. It is always the last to be sung and is almost a lullaby to us. It is known as Shenandoah.

I smiled at your first question, Meg. You were always interested in babies. Yes, to answer your question there are very young babies, three of them and four women that I know of who are pregnant. It always amazes me that relatively young children will have set jobs to do. Often an older child will care for a baby or another child when their Mother is driving the wagon. I am only learning now how to care for a baby and that is only by watching. I don't think they trust me to care for their babies. Yet these children hitch a baby into their arms or a youngster on to their hip. Later the mother is to be seen walking along with the babe at her breast and young children holding on to her skirts. They are wonderful women. All have a terrible fear of snakes. Many have started to tie their younger children to a rope, which in turn is tied to her apron strings. The child can't wander into the prairie or stop to pick up a snake or a scorpion. I love to see them pattering along and I know that you would. They remind me of a duck and her string of ducklings.

No, no, no, I am not going to make you an aunt. I find this journey hard enough to cope with without pregnancy or a baby.

This wagon train is not the perfect heaven on earth that you seem to think Meg. There are arguments at times, usually between the same two men and nearly always on a baking hot, stressful day. It amounts to shouting and threats, a couple of times fisticuffs and on one never to be forgotten day a gun was drawn. A fist from Mr Nesbitt soon put a stop to that. Most of the women get along with each other, sometimes there is a raised voice but it soon quietens. I think they feel ashamed at showing their irritation.

I've tried to answer all your questions, now you should answer mine. I worry about you and all the family. How is your cough, are you able to sit out of bed for longer periods. Does Mama tell you what Dr Harris says? Is Mr Osbourne calling to see you?. I liked him very much. Hurry and get well, I need you to tell me about all the concerts and to collect all the gossip!

Are Mama and Papa well? I try to think what you all will be doing. Mama will be busy organising the gardener. Papa, busy trying to keep out of Mama's way by going for walks in Central Park three times a day, and you? You, Meg, will be sat there observing everything, missing nothing and remembering it all and I want to know it all!

Meg, after the last twenty four hours we are in a sorry state. There has been storm after storm like nothing I have ever seen. The sky was ripped by lightning, dozens of streaks at the same time. The thunder seemed to bounce off the earth and then career around the sky only to crash into another peal. The rain was a huge waterfall that filled the sky. Children and more than one woman was crying and wailing. Even the men admitted to being frightened. They spent over twenty hours out in it pacifying and trying to stop the animals stampeding. Two cows were struck and killed by lightning. It seems a miracle that we all survived it. Everything we have is saturated, bedding, clothes, provisions, the floors of the wagons are like lakes. We are attempting to salvage what we can and more than one soul has tears streaming down their faces. Most of the women are trying to make flat bread from lumps of soaking wet flour, wet coffee is being moulded into small bricks and put in the sun to dry. Others are just throwing it away! Mr Nesbitt has warned that we need to rescue every ounce of provisions as there are hungry time in front of us.

Martha soon had a group of children around her as she tried to squeeze water out of everything she possessed and started singing all the nonsense songs that she seems to have an endless store of. The children are quick learners and were soon roaring them out and a lot of their parents joined in. Zack started to dance with one of the children and everyone clapped and cheered. Then Seth who doesn't like to be left out of anything started to do a chicken walk and went flat on his back in the mud. Then there was a mad ten minutes, people danced, smeared mud on each other's faces and laughed hysterically at anyone and anything. Then sense, of a sort, returned. Somehow the rain didn't seem so wet or the mud so thick, we realised that it wasn't the end of the world. I think that ten minutes of madness will stay with me all my life.

Today is Sunday and a rest day. There is bedding and clothes hung out to dry everywhere. Every item that should be in the wagon is in the sun with the steam rising from it. Then we are faced with the hard job of re-packing it. Mr Nesbitt has been working with everyone. Some have resented his advice of abandoning most if not all their furniture. John and I have stood amazed at what has been unloaded. Harmoniums, ploughs, wardrobes, fire stoves and everyone except us has their marriage bed with them. He has warned everyone that there are very difficult days in front of us and the wagons need to be as light as possible or the oxen may not survive.

We are heading for Independence Rock but it will take us weeks to get there. I am told that there is every danger in front of us ranging from treacherous rivers to warring tribes of Indians.

I think we are all dreading the next stage.

Bless you dear sister and pray for us all

Your loving sister
Isabelle.

August 1849

My Dearest Sister,

You have been in my thoughts so much recently. It isn't just the fact that you are getting married and I won't be there, but the fact that I will never see you or Mama and Papa again. I am so homesick, Meg. We are travelling through wonderful country but all I want is the noise and dirt of New York. My life is with John and I must go where he goes but that doesn't stop me longing for home. I am so sorry for being miserable. I'll stop and write in a few days time when hopefully my spirit will be brighter.

One week later.
Did I tell you that I am learning to knit and am fast learning that I should keep to fine embroidery. Greta who is Dutch decided she would teach me. She has a huge sack full of wool and I chose a lovely pink hank. I was soon told that it was too fine to learn to knit with and was given one more suitable for making a fishing net! That was just the start of my troubles. Not knowing anything about wool or knitting I wound it too tight, dropped the needles, the ball of wool was on the ground more than in my lap. Then the stitches developed a life of their own and kept jumping off the needles. Greta realised that I was trying to follow her left- handed way of working! Things did improve a little after that but not a lot. I was the group's entertainment for a couple of hours and they don't think that I will progress further than patchwork squares!

We arrived at Independence Rock a few days ago, four weeks later than planned. We have had problems with wagons, people and livestock and now we are getting short of provisions. The Rock is like a giant overturned turtle. For some reason the custom has developed among the pioneers to leave their names on the rock. John is always saying that we learn something new every day and today it was how to mix gunpowder, bison grease and tar into a paint. I don't know that we will ever use that knowledge again, but as John said, we have it. I spent a couple of hours printing names so that that everyone could copy their name on to the rock. They were mighty pleased with themselves. I stood reading some of the names and wondered if they would still be there in a hundred years.

Martha has delivered two more babies in the last few weeks, both boys. It is the only time that she has come alive and out of the closed world she has retreated into. She blames her husband Zack for their child's death and he blames himself. They have no comfort for each other, Meg. Verity, the second woman to be delivered is ill. There were complications with the birth. Mr Nesbitt has agreed to a few days rest here although there are mutterings from the usual people. I think deep down most of us are glad of the rest.

Late August.

Dear Meg,

I'm sorry I couldn't write from Fort Bridger. We have had an outbreak of cholera and I thought I was going to die. Many of us would have only for the kindness of a group of Snake Indians but more of that later. Nobody escaped it and we were all devastated when Verity, her baby and one of the young men died within twenty hours of each other. We were shocked and frightened. Every morning and every evening we found ourselves silently counting heads and thanking God we were still alive.

When we finally reached Fort Bridger nobody was allowed in to it. Mr Nesbitt had to shout over the stockade what supplies we needed. Our money was then put into a bucket of vinegar, which was left outside the gate for twelve hours. The store would not accept paper money and because we had little in coins, demanded a cow. It was a poor, thin, specimen but the best we had, they then demanded another one! Supplies, which were of poor quality, inadequate and expensive, were placed outside the gate the following morning.

We were then threatened and forced to move on. I can understand them being frightened of cholera, but they showed us no Christian kindness.

Then we had the strangest of experiences, Meg. Everyone was so ill that we could only travel a mile or so from the fort. Unhitching the oxen was the most we had the strength to do for any of the beasts. We just dropped under the nearest bush or tree. We knew that we wouldn't get out of the wagon and make it to the bushes in time if nature called. Most of us were curled up into balls when a voice urgent with panic and fear screamed Oh my God, Mr Nesbitt, Mr Nesbitt!

We dragged our heads up to see a group of mounted Indians staring at us from the side of our wagons. We had no means of defending ourselves and do you know, Meg, I don't think one of us cared if we lived or died. They watched silently as Mr Nesbitt and John dragged themselves to their feet. They watched as John clutched his belly and doubled up in pain and Mr Nesbitt tried to steady himself and walk towards them. They listened, unmoved as he struggled to speak. The air was still, silent, even the birds and trees seemed to be holding their breath. One of their group swung off his horse and came towards us. It was our turn to stare, stare unbelievingly at his dark, wooden leg as it swung so easily, backwards and forward. We stared at its finial of woven grass and leather and listened to the soft muffled tap as it touched the ground. He stopped, and in perfect English asked if we needed help. We were dumbstruck. Mr Nesbitt was the first to gather his voice and wits and quickly explained our predicament. Then as he said later, his tongue ran away with him.

Are you Peg-Leg Grant? I thought someone had imagined you, a myth.

I was Saul Grant, but live with and have been known to this tribe as One Leg for many years.

At that time we were too ill to be curious about his story, but later was a different matter.

It was to be over a week before One Leg and his companion left us. The rest of their group continued their hunting trip after they had filled our water barrels and brought roots, herbs and grasses from their village. The two men stayed near us but not with us. Within a short time they were rubbing and pounding herbs together. They mixed the powder with water and gave precise instructions on how it was to be taken. Jonas Appleyard, one of our usual grumblers, said that we would be poisoned. I must confess it crossed all our minds after tasting the bitter brew. Within a few days we could hardly believe the improvement in most of us. Although still ill and weak, the camp started to live again. We woke one morning to find them gone. We couldn't believe that they would go without us having a chance to thank them. Then at noon they were back with us. One Leg had been to their village and brought corn flour for us to make gruel. Red Wing returned with a dozen large salmon that he had caught. In what seemed minutes they were gutted, cut into slivers and threaded on sticks to dry in the sun.

How can you thank complete strangers for saving so many lives, Meg? They started to make their goodbyes when John dashed into the wagon and came out with his waistcoats and presented them to them. It was obvious that they were pleased, so he dashed in again and came out with my two hats dangling by their ribbons. I had hung them to one of the struts of the wagon just to remind me of my other life. Meg, you should have seen the smiles on their faces, they couldn't take their eyes of them. Everyone tried to give them something but apart from that clothing all they would take was a tin cup and plate each. So my dear Sister, I will go into Oregon without a hat to my name. Mama would have a fainting fit if she knew.

We are in the Rockies and travelling is much easier than we thought it would be. It is so beautiful, Meg. Wherever your eyes rest there are green forests, snow capped mountains, blue skies, and even more snow capped mountains. The air is so clear and bright it teases your nose and polishes your eyes. And over it all is that special smell of thousands of fir trees. Everywhere there is the sound of running water from rivers, cascades, streams and whirlpools. As beautiful as it is, there is a darker side. The wagons are not as spread as usual, the children are kept close and rifles are carried the whole time. We are always guarding against brown bears, grizzly bears and mountain lions. Mr Nesbitt said that they know no fear especially the grizzly. The night watch has been doubled after wolves were heard. I don't know which is greater our fear of Indians or wild animals!

In the distance we can see our next destination, Fort Hall and we will be so glad to get there in a few days. Our provisions are very low.

Has Mama stopped inviting the top layer of society to your wedding? John and I have laughed so often at the stories you have told us. Has anyone refused an invitation? I don't think they would dare. It would be wiser to jump into the Hudson River than cross Mama! Poor Papa, when you are gone he will get the full organising attention of Mama! No doubt he will be down at his club half of the time and the other half playing deaf!

Oh what a woeful letter this has been, my dear sister. Take care of yourself, Meg. I think of you so much.

All my love.
Isabelle.

September 1849

My Dearest Sister,

You can't imagine my joy on receiving your lovely, fat, squashy letter at Fort Hall. As soon as I touched it I knew it would be the one topic of conversation for days. I felt like a criminal as I tried to flit between the wagons without being stopped. I wanted to read and savour your letter by myself, without a dozen expectant faces gazing at me. I'm so glad that I did. Tears started to roll as soon as I saw the sketches of your wedding dress. It is so lovely and you will look wonderful. I've read your letter again and again and cried even more. I feel our journey will be ending as your new life is starting.

Meg, you have no idea of the excitement the fabrics and sketches created with the women. They have been studied from every angle. I was so glad that you included the back views of both your dress and going away suit. The women were amazed at the intricate work in the backs of both of them. Dora and Kate demanded to know what this drape or that pleat was called and how it was achieved. They should have known better than to ask me! John had the solution. He spent an hour or more moving our possessions until he managed to haul my trunk out and then the fun really started. Every item of clothing was examined inside and out, the quality of the fabric, the styling, the stitching, all were studied and commented on. Honestly Meg, I learnt more about my clothing than I had ever known. Dora very hesitantly asked if she could unpick small areas of the lining to see how the different effects had been achieved. Within minutes she and Kate were practising what they saw. Aprons, towels and anything else they could find were pleated, folded and compared to the garment. Already they are talking about setting up a dressmaking shop. I told them that in New York if they intended it to be high-class establishment it would be called a salon. As Kate remarked, Oregon won't always be a frontier territory and in time, more than spades, kettles and coffins would be wanted. For a whole evening it was the only topic of conversation with the women. They all realised the importance of the right salon name but some of the suggestions caused hysterics. It really lifted our spirits. I have been given the task of listing ALL of New York's salons. There are going to be many enjoyable evenings spent on this task.

I could see John's mind ticking over during these conversations and, of course, a question here and there. I am sure he will offer to finance the venture for a percentage of the business or profits! See Meg, I am getting to know how businesses work. He is like his father, able to recognise opportunities.

There was one thing I realised when I saw my New York clothes. What an implement of torture a pair of corsets is. I don't think I can ever wear them again!

Oh Meg, what am I thinking, I haven't thanked you for your long newsy letter. It was so good to hear all the gossip and potted versions of all the concerts, plays and balls you've been too. It seems like another world, especially when I'm hauling water out of a river or trudging mile after dusty mile.

Isn't Mama exasperating? I should imagine the poor milliner's heart sinks when she sees Mama walking in her direction. I can just hear Mama justifying her sharp tongue, I'm not being rude to the woman, I just have high standards. Then giving the poor woman her sweetest smile. She will never change.

Fort Hall is like every other trading post we have been to. Short of basic provisions and unwilling to sell to anyone who isn't a trapper. There have been arguments and threats made by some of the men towards the manager of the fort. Mr Nesbitt has had difficulty in smoothing the situation. In the end we got a small amount but not nearly enough for our needs. Once again we will be relying on what we can find or snare on the way.

The wagon train is smaller now. At Fort Hall we parted with those going south to California. It was upsetting to see so many good friends leaving. It was also a relief to see others go. We have had trouble with two men from soon after we started. Really, it is one man, who for some unknown reason decided that he was going to make the other man's life hell. They have argued, fought and made life difficult for each other and their families. The general feeling is that only one will survive to see California.

We are thankful that the people we are closest to have their eyes set on Oregon.

John and Zack have had their heads together a lot in the last few weeks.

So much so that Zack and his family have changed their plans and are now coming to Oregon. John has so many ideas for the future and Zack is a big part of them. I am so grateful that Martha will be near.

Yes, the reading and writing lessons are continuing, but the nights are drawing in and there is neither time nor light after we stop for the night. They can all write their names and most quite a lot more. As they have progressed with writing, learning to read has become a burning ambition with them. How I wish I had our childhood books here, books are unheard of on the trail. I love working with them all. From the oldest to the youngest they are so keen to learn. I have told John that I am determined to open a school. His reply? Start planning it.

Oh Meg, you made our mouths water with the menu for your wedding breakfast. We are all so tired and sick of salt bacon and beef. We laughed at the thought of Mama hiring French chefs, and then I had to explain to my friends what a French chef did! I can imagine Cook's thoughts on that. I bet Papa won't let anyone near his cellar and has the key hidden away from Uncle James! Do you remember how drunk he was at my wedding and how annoyed Papa was. I'm surprised that Mama will let him in the house!

John has bought his first parcels of land. Three Italian families arrived at the fort the day before we were leaving. They had farmed their allocation of land in Oregon for the three years to make it legally theirs but just couldn't settle. They had been neighbours in Italy so decided to try their luck in California. So we now have the deeds to three adjoining parcels of land. Every spare second John and Zack are studying the deeds and maps, planning this, that and the other.

Mid September.

My dearest Sister,

The day after your wedding we arrived in Oregon and what a dreadful shock it was. We looked in vain for the lush pastures, the trees, the rivers. Where was the land of plenty? All we found was a vast land, barren and dry, without a tree, stream or any grazing. All that was growing was sage bushes, too tough for the livestock to eat. Even though there isn't a grain of sand on it, it is known as the High Desert. It took three days of torture to cross it Meg, The animals were in a terrible state, some died and I felt that we hadn't the right to put them through this. When I said this to John he answered that many had put their children through it.

We came out of this hell into the Oregon territory of our hopes. Plentiful pasture and a river known as the Sweet River and it certainly was. We left it reluctantly three days later, refreshed and in better spirits. We are making for the trading post at a place called The Dalles. It is our last stop and we are faced with a difficult, frightening decision before we start the final stage to Oregon City.

Meg, please do send me a pressed flower from your bouquet. I know it is a foolish request. I forget when I am writing to you that it may be weeks or even months before you receive it. It would be something to remember your wedding by.

Take care of yourself, my dearest sister. Tell Samuel that I welcome him as my new brother-in- law.

Your loving sister,
Isabelle

October 1849

We have arrived! After all these months we are in Oregon City. The journey is over and I can't believe that we are here safely.

My Dear, Dear Sister,

I don't know where to begin, so much has and is happening. I think the best place is where my last letter finished. We made faster time to The Dalles than we had hoped and prayed for. With only half the number of wagons and less than half the livestock it was a lot easier than we had expected. Reaching the Dalles trading post meant there was one last big decision to be made. It hung over us from leaving the prairies. Do we travel on the new trail around Mt Hood or the faster way down the Columbia River? Mr Nesbitt urged us all to take the mountain way and as you can imagine this didn't please everyone. The river passage would entail the building of huge rafts, loading our wagons on to them and travelling more than a hundred miles on what he described as the most ferocious river in the land. Meg, my heart froze. I couldn't imagine anything worse than the rivers we had already crossed. I'm sure I would have walked to Oregon City by myself sooner than face the river that had claimed so many lives. Mr. Nesbitt said he would continue with those willing to follow his advice and the rest must see to themselves. As John said, we haven't travelled all these miles and months to lose our lives for the sake of another week. Only one family has gone to the river and it was not the choice of Lizzie or her five children. They were terrified and clung to us as they said their goodbyes. The snow was starting to fall as we made for the trail around Mt. Hood. It was breathtaking but hard work for both beasts and people. Some of the adults and children had never seen snow in their whole life. We have a Polish pioneer family who soon showed us ways of staying warm. We had dried grass packed into shoes, bonnets, and the children between their underclothing as well. We were so glad of it!

I can't describe our feelings when the Willamette valley opened out in front of us. The next day we got our first glimpse of Oregon City. The men clasped each other, the women hugged anyone and everyone, and most of us cried and cried. It was strange how quiet and exhausted we all became then. John said the word to describe us was drained, and as usual he was right.

I don't know what I expected from Oregon City but a city it certainly isn't. Wooden shacks, three saloons, two small general stores, a lodging house, half a bank, (the rest being built) a gaol and a coffin maker, makes up the hub of this city. Yet it seemed so crowded and smelly after the last six months travelling in the wide-open space of prairie, desert, and mountain.

There are quite a few families facing the winter in their wagons. They arrived too late to occupy their land, to fell timber and build their cabin. We are in the happy position of having cabins and a good woodpile on the three parcels of land that John bought or so we were assured. They have already visited the Land Office and should be allocated their land within a few weeks. Everywhere, there are questions to be asked about crops, livestock, weather. They pore over maps for hours. Both have an air of excitement about them and seem ready for any challenge. We arrived twenty-four hours ago and already they have gone to check the land and cabins. We have no idea where the cabins are or when they are likely to be back. Tomorrow, next week, next month, I have a feeling this is going to be our life for a few months.

Martha and I have had the wonderful task of buying stores. We stood like children staring in wonderment at provisions we haven't seen in six months. Writing paper, ink, molasses, hats and bonnets, crockery that isn't tin and to my delight, candy. I stood and ate a slab of chocolate, then I had another. I have longed for the taste of it since we started this journey. Without Martha I would have had no idea of the range of essentials we would need. I swear salted and dried bacon or meat will never be on my table. A year ago I would have laughed at the idea that buying provisions could be more pleasurable than choosing a new hat. In fact I would have laughed at the idea of me buying provisions.

Our next stop was the coffin maker who also makes very basic furniture. It doesn't matter what you ask for, it all looks the same, four legs joined by a plank! I couldn't help recalling all the lovely furniture that Pioneers had been forced to leave on the banks of rivers and at the foot of cliffs. They must long for it now.

Oh Meg, I am so sorry. I've been babbling away without asking about you and all the family news. I am longing to hear it. Is your house ready or are you still living with Samuel's parents? I'm sure that by the time you receive this letter you will be entertaining the families who matter in New York. I can imagine Mama as the mother of the hostess. She will bestow a smile here, a word there and be quite regal as she sails around. All Papa will want is the card table! I don't let myself think of New York Meg, except when I write to you. Then I can smell and hear it. There are times when the longing to walk its streets and see and talk to you is an unbearable ache. Oh dear this will never do. I'll change the subject.

Now, to our wonderful news. I was determined to finish this letter on a happy note instead of all the fears I seem to have ended with in the last months. You have got your wish. I'm going to have a baby. You are going to be an aunt. I can imagine that smile spreading all over your face. It is due April/May time. Please don't mention it to Mama until I have written to her. Martha who has a saying for every occasion keeps saying, New house, new baby.

She and all her family will be living in one of the cabins and has promised to deliver the babe.

John is thrilled and very proud of himself. He had it all planned, as soon as labour started he would ride into town for the doctor, and also hire a nurse for the six weeks after the birth. Then he found out there was neither nurse nor doctor in the town, apart from Mr Jack the horse doctor. Gossiping with the Pioneer women, there is not one who has had a doctor to deliver their babies. I insisted that I wanted Martha and no one else to deliver our child.

It has amused all the women on the wagon train how he has fussed, coddled and embarrassed me. They all swear that if they married again it would be to a man from New York!

I really am going to have to learn to knit now, otherwise this poor child will be born without a stitch to wear.

We have been in Oregon City twenty-four hours and already Dora and Kate have started to earn money for food and their dream salon. Two barrels, one plank, two little sewing machines sitting on it and two stools. A line of men, some without shirts, some holding their trousers in front of them all waiting to have and pay for repairs. I think a lot of the men in Oregon must be unmarried. Dora and Kate have what served as their mattress between them and it is stuffed full of pieces of fabric. They have really impressed John with their planning. If possible can you send me any pictures, or drawings of fashion, hats, gloves or bags, anything that you think may be of use to them.

Please write soon, dear sister. I know there will be letters on the way to me but as you know they can take months to arrive. Tell me the small happenings as well as the large important ones, most of all tell me about you.

Your loving sister
Isabelle.

The Delivery

Delivery

I answered the knock. I recognised the small brown parcel in the postman's hand. My neighbours had lived this moment before me. I signed for it. Are you alright, missus?

I sat in the chair gazing into the fire. It was one of his favourite pastimes as a child, making fire pictures. Castles, volcanoes, shipwrecks, they were all there. But all I can see is shell holes, trenches and that hell, the Somme. My chest is tight, I can hardly breathe.

Missing – presumed dead. No known grave.

His boots stand side-by-side on the hearthstone. I can't bring myself to move them. They are my act of faith, my touchstone. They'll be ready waiting for him when he comes home.

He always sat on the back step, whistling, as he blacked them and I cherish his quick smile, the set of his head, his hands. It's all I've got. A pair of boots and a ladder of birthday notches on the outhouse door.

Just like his mates, he couldn't wait to go. What did the posters say?

Work together – fight together. Aye, and this street knows the price of that.

I open the parcel. Two medals and a brass plaque.

A brass plaque for our golden lad. A slip of paper.

The King wishes me … gave his life that others might live.

It chokes me. I didn't notice any of your sons, George, being led by donkeys in Flanders mud, with trench foot, shell shock, making the supreme sacrifice.

The only consolation I can cling to is that no one else will suffer this pain. That this is the war to end all wars.